TO SERVE THE
PRESENT AGE

TO SERVE THE PRESENT AGE

The Brethren Service Story

by

M. R. Zigler

and other former participants

Donald F. Durnbaugh, editor

The Brethren Press
Elgin, Ill.

Library of Congress Cataloging in Publication Data
Main entry under title:

To serve the present age.

    Bibliography: p.
    1. Church of the Brethren. Brethren Service Commis-
sion. 2. Church of the Brethren—Charities.
3. World War, 1939-1945—Civilian relief. I. Zigler,
M. R. II. Durnbaugh, Donald F.
BX7827.3.T6   266'.65   75-6633
ISBN 0-87178-848-9

Contents

Photo Sources

David Briggs, 99
Church World Service, 95
El Mundo, 81 bottom
Ora Huston, 100 top
J. Henry Long, 83 bottom, 84 bottom, 86 bottom, 89, 90, 92 top, 94 top, 97 top, 100 bottom
Michigan State University Information Services, 97 bottom
Photo-Hilfswerk, 84 top, 85
Merlin G. Shull, 98 bottom
U.S. Information Service, 77, 93 bottom
Leland Wilson, 93 top
All others from Brethren Service Commission and General Board files

Cover design Ken Stanley

Contributors

M. R. ZIGLER. Formerly Executive, Brethren Service Commission, Brethren Service Commission in the United States and Europe; Representative of the Church of the Brethren to the Federal and World Council of Churches. Currently in retirement at Sebring, Florida, and Broadway, Virginia

ELDON R. BURKE. Formerly Professor of History, Ball State University; Director of CRALOG, Germany; Professor of History, Manchester College. Currently Professor of History, St. Francis College, Fort Wayne, Indiana

DONALD F. DURNBAUGH. Formerly Director, Brethren Service Program in Austria. Currently Professor of Church History, Bethany Theological Seminary, Oak Brook, Illinois

JOHN H. EBERLY. Formerly School Administrator, Indiana; Brethren Service Commission, Italy and Germany; Director, Student Exchange Program; Director, Brethren Service Center, New Windsor, Maryland; Pastor, Maryland. Currently in retirement at Sebring, Florida

MARY COPPOCK HAMMOND. Formerly Director, International Work Camp Programs, Europe. Currently teaching in Warner-Robbins, Georgia

LUTHER H. HARSHBARGER. Formerly Senior Representative, World's YMCA Prisoners' Aid in Belgium, the Netherlands, and Germany; University Chaplain, Pennsylvania State University. Currently Professor of Humanities and Religious Studies, Pennsylvania State University, University Park, Pennsylvania

THURL METZGER. Formerly Brethren Service Commission representative, Poland; Executive Secretary, Heifer Project, International. Currently Director of International Programs, Heifer Project International, Little Rock, Arkansas

JOHN D. METZLER, SR. Formerly Director, Brethren Service Center, New Windsor, Maryland; Executive Secretary, CROP; Senior Staff Member, World Council of Churches; District Executive, Church of the Brethren. Currently in retirement at Fruitland, Idaho

ORIE O. MILLER. Formerly Executive Secretary, Mennonite Central Committee; Secretary, Mennonite Board of Missions and Charities. Currently in retirement at Lititz, Pennsylvania

JOSEPH B. MOW. Formerly with the UNRRA/Brethren Service Tractor Unit, China; Resettlement Officer, World Council of Churches Service to Refugees; Resettlement Officer, Church World Service. Currently Professor of Philosophy and Religion, West Virginia Wesleyan College, Buckhannon, West Virginia

BYRON P. ROYER. Formerly Brethren Service Commission Representative, Germany; Pastor, Illinois. Currently Professor of Pastoral Psychology, Bethany Theological Seminary, Oak Brook, Illinois

LAWRENCE W. SHULTZ. Formerly Professor and Librarian, Manchester College; Chairman, Brethren Service Committee; Manager, Camp Mack; Director, Brethren Tours. Currently in retirement, North Manchester, Indiana

MARY BLOCHER SMELTZER. Formerly Brethren Service Committee Representative, Japanese Relocation Project; Educator, Illinois. Currently teaching in Washington, D.C.

RALPH E. SMELTZER. Formerly Director, Brethren Service Program in Austria; Brethren Service Commission Staff, Elgin, Illinois. Currently Washington Representative, Church of the Brethren, Washington, D.C.

HOWARD E. SOLLENBERGER. Formerly Director, UNRRA/Brethren Service Tractor Unit, China. Currently Director, Foreign Service Institute, Department of State, Washington, D.C.

OPAL D. STECH. Formerly Brethren Service Commission Representative, Poland; Professor of Home Economics, Manchester College. Currently in retirement at North Manchester, Indiana

GRANT M. STOLTZFUS. Formerly Director, Civilian Public Service Camp, Maryland; Professor of Anthropology, Eastern Mennonite College. Deceased

DAN WEST. Formerly Relief Worker, American Friends Service Committee, Spain; Originator, Heifer Project; Peace Representative, Church of the Brethren. Deceased

Introduction

by Donald F. Durnbaugh

A recent book describing the relief and rehabilitation work of American voluntary agencies in Germany after World War II begins with a quotation from M. R. Zigler. The Brethren Service leader had managed to visit the devastated, Allied-occupied nation (as one of the first churchmen allowed entry) with the intent of examining needs and reporting them to the American churches. One of many poignant incidents he experienced was a conversation with a Berlin mother:

"The woman announced without apparent emotion that she must decide which of her children she would try to keep alive during the winter to come. She could not possibly find enough food for all four of her children, and she had to choose which one or two had the best chances of surviving. The food she scrounged would go to them and she would have to watch the others waste away.... It was reported from Berlin that during the winter most of the children under three failed to survive."

Veteran Brethren Service worker John W. Barwick wrote in the *Gospel Messenger* in February, 1946, comparing needs in Germany with the rest of Western Europe. The latter countries were by that time well on the way to recovery, owing to massive foreign aid and the sturdy will of the people to rebuild. Barwick reported:

"Germany today looks rather like, though worse than, Holland a year ago. The large cities and the Ruhr district are concentrations of ravenous people.... The fact that starvation exists on an incredible scale in even the American zone has been documented by so many accounts of reliable witnesses, I shall not tell more. Frankly, the psychosis of most allies in Germany worries me more. Four soldiers with whom I rode in a truck turned in a road to an air strip. At the intersection, the corpse of a baby lay on the trunk of an uprooted tree. Nobody, except the woman moaning over it, paid more than the

Introduction

slightest attention. I watched two soldiers detailed to take a load of corpses, all nothing but skeletons with tight skin stretched over them, to the 'pit,' as the local burying ground was called. They chatted and smoked and finally one rubbed his cigarette out on a shrunken foot protruding from the rear of the truck. The callousness of ordinary Americans to frightful need and starving thousands about them must be seen to be believed."

The relief and rehabilitation work of the Brethren Service Commission (BSC) had a dual focus: the first was to send material aid—food, clothes, medicine—to those in dire need, even to those former enemies such as the Germans. The second, made necessary by the first, was to appeal to the conscience of the membership of the Church of the Brethren. For the most part, Brethren had not been directly touched by the impact of the war and its aftermath. The response was impressive. During the fiscal year ending February 28, 1947, the value of materials administered and distributed reached $7,189,000, although not all of this was contributed directly by Brethren. The administrative cost was less than two percent. The work done at that time earned for the Brethren a reputation for concern and effectiveness.

In a review of a book by Harold E. Fey on the work of Church World Service (CWS) from 1946 to 1966, D. Elton Trueblood remarked on the activity of "some of the smaller denominations, particularly the Mennonites and the Brethren." Trueblood commented: "When I talked to my wife about the tremendous record of the Brethren as Fey reports it, she replied that they didn't have to spend money on cathedrals.... Christ is not reported to have said anything about the duty of erecting fine structures, but he is reported as saying, 'As you did it to one of the least of these my brethren, you did it to me'" (*Christian Century*, July 20, 1966). This comment catches very well the spirit of the Brethren during and immediately after the Second World War.

Today when some Brethren congregations are building neo-Georgian edifices of cathedral-like proportions and cost, and when Brethren Service-type activity is more limited, it is worthwhile to recall the beginnings of BSC work. There are many current members of the Church of the Brethren who have never heard the story; others may have forgotten it. The intent of this volume is neither to engage in self-congratulatory exercises nor to indulge in nostalgia. Rather, the editor and contributors hope this recounting might help to provide nerve and muscle for meeting current problems. At a time when world hunger is reaching great magnitude, such a retelling may inspire Brethren to efforts comparable to those achieved earlier. Such is the hope of this book.

The book belongs to M. R. Zigler. For several years he urged that a collection be made of firsthand reports of the early years of BSC. Some of the pioneer workers have already died—Dan West, John W. Barwick, W. Harold Row, Lorell Weiss, and others—and their stories went with them. Zigler drew up a tentative outline of the book, listing those who he thought should be appropriately included. He enlisted the aid of Dan Raffensperger and Don Durnbaugh, both former BSC workers in Europe, to bring the project to fruition. These two, with the counsel of Kenneth I. Morse of the Brethren Press, developed further plans for the book. A grant from Dan Raffensperger ensured its publication.

By happy chance, the editor discovered in the files of the General Offices of the Church of the Brethren in Elgin, Illinois, a manuscript dictated by M. R. Zigler after his return from Europe in 1958. He was aided in its compilation by Frances Clemens Nyce and Suzanne Windisch in Europe, and by Edith Bonsack Barnes in Elgin. Several chapters from the longer study appeared to be helpful in presenting an overview of BSC work, with particular attention to the philosophy and approach which characterized BSC operations. The first part of the book, then, consists of portions of a larger unpublished document. Its function is to provide the frame for the mosaic of individual stories.

Contributors were asked to put down their thoughts and memories of the early years; they were not to write documented histories but rather to give personal, human-interest accounts of what seemed significant after these two or three decades. The response was gratifying. The volunteering spirit which took these men and women from family and familiar surroundings to sites of discomfort, stress, and occasional danger is reflected in their willingness to produce, without remuneration, essays on their experiences. Not surprisingly, the memories refer more to the achievements and joys than to the failures and frustrations, but some of the accounts do chronicle also the problems and difficulties inherent in the jobs.

By design, Brethren Service workers were sent on short-term assignments rarely over three years in length. This means that the projects and programs here described were staffed by many different people over the years. Those writing here are typically the persons who began the work. Later staff members continued, expanded, and changed as necessary what had been begun. These later personnel are not mentioned, but this should not be interpreted as evidence that their work was of lesser importance or not worthy of recognition. It was simply not possible to list everyone.

As might be expected in a book of this type, it was necessary to make painful choices and to allow some regrettable omissions. Because the plan of the book parallels M. R. Zigler's major responsibilities with BSC, important segments of Brethren activity are neglected. There was a great amount of relief work carried on in India and China, at times under direct BSC auspices, by Brethren mission personnel. This is not covered. Portions of that story are available elsewhere, particularly in writings on Brethren missions. Another example is the case study of mass employment for relief conducted by Brethren mission personnel in Northern India in 1942. This is described in Hertha Kraus, *International Relief in Action (1914-1943),* a book produced by the Philadelphia research center established by the historic peace churches during World War II in preparation for relief work after the end of the war.

Brethren Service also carried on comprehensive programs in social action and social education, with particular emphasis upon peace. These are not reported in this book except for passing mention. The short-term nature of many projects in these fields makes description difficult by means of memoirs. They were effective and reached thousands of people.

Under the leadership of W. Harold Row, Brethren Service work was continued and, in some respects, expanded. Several important projects and programs developed during his administration are not reported at all in this volume. The work of the International Voluntary Service teams around the world, the interchange between the Church of the Brethren and the Russian Orthodox Church—these and other developments must be left to a later chronicler.

To Serve the Present Age

Finally, it must be stressed that this is by no means the total BSC story. It intends to be a contribution to that story. It should help document and undergird a more substantial study which needs to be written. By preserving reactions and memories of a score of former BSC staff, it will in its own way provide a service for Brethren and others interested.

Abbreviations Used in the Text

AFSC	American Friends Service Committee
AGREHAB	Agricultural Rehabilitation Division (UNRRA)
BSC	Brethren Service Committee (later Brethren Service Commission)
BSU	Brethren Service Unit
BVS	Brethren Volunteer Service
BYPD	Brethren Young People's Department
CARE	Cooperative for American Remittances to Europe (later Cooperative for American Relief Everywhere)
CCC	Civilian Conservation Corps
CNRRA	Chinese National Reconstruction and Rehabilitation Administration
CO	Conscientious Objector
CPS	Civilian Public Service
CRALOG	Council of Relief Agencies Licensed for Operation in Germany
CROP	Christian Rural Overseas Program
CWS	Church World Service
DP	Displaced Person
FAO	Food and Agriculture Organization
FOR	Fellowship of Reconciliation
HICOG	High Commissioner for the Occupation of Germany
HPC	Historic Peace Churches
HPI	Heifer Project International
ICYE	International Christian Youth Exchange
IFOR	International Fellowship of Reconciliation
IRO	International Refugee Organization
JACL	Japanese American Citizens League
LWF	Lutheran World Federation
MCC	Mennonite Central Committee
NSBRO	National Service Board for Religious Objectors
POW	Prisoner of War
UNESCO	United Nations Educational, Scientific, and Cultural Organization
UNRRA	United Nations Relief and Rehabilitation Administration
WCC	World Council of Churches
WRA	War Relocation Authority
YMCA	Young Men's Christian Association

PART ONE
THE BRETHREN SERVICE STORY

1. The Discovery of Persons

by M. R. Zigler

People everywhere were stunned at the announcement of events which led to a second world war. It was the general belief that the war should have been avoided. There had been promises by men and by governments earlier that there would not be another war. Incident after incident occurred that was tied directly or indirectly to what became the slogan, "This war is the war to end war." Directly or indirectly men desperately dedicated their lives for the making of peace by promoting and participating heartily in carnal warfare.

In the United States the Mennonites, Friends, and Brethren had been meeting through the years. They came together occasionally to discuss issues, always assuring each other that there would be nothing binding on the part of the three bodies. The subject matter for the meetings was carefully "agendized" so that there would be no criticism about those who met or against the sponsoring bodies. This was carried through on a national level, but seldom did Mennonites, Friends, or Brethren meet together in local communities to discuss the same problems explored by representatives on the national level.

Through this fellowship in conference, a sense of trust had been developed between those who participated, as persons for the most part rather than as officials representing their churches. When the United States government made the official call for men to enter the armed forces for "dedication unto death," and for the magnificent objective of justice and peace on earth, the historic peace churches realized their need for common action to stand together at the point of agreeing not to participate in war.

Attention by all three groups centered on the Selective Service Act of 1940. Each group proceeded to find a way through to a satisfactory understanding not only on the part of the relationship of the historic peace churches and the government, but also between the historic peace churches and other religious bodies that did not take the peace position of nonviolence. They were faced also with the problem of meeting the ultranationalistic groups and individuals who emphasized above all else loyalty to the nation.

It was clear without discussion that there would have to be a united, creative fellowship to use all strength available and every new insight possible to meet the inevitable issues. There was a sense of need for each other. A meeting was called in Chicago on October 4-5, 1940, at which, for the first time since the division of 1880, all Brethren bodies met, this time with the Mennonites and the Friends. All these got together in a Mennonite mission church to decide on a unified approach of the historic peace churches to government in all its relationships. At this meeting with the representatives of the Brethren churches were Orie Miller of the Mennonites and Ray Newton and Ray Wilson of the Friends. Charles Boss of the Methodists met with the group to become aware of what the historic peace churches were doing for conscientious objectors. There were conscientious objectors within the Methodist fellowship.

A committee was authorized to go to Washington to follow through on behalf of all persons who would take an honest stand against war as a method of settling the world's problems. Acting together in a fellowship with a common cause, these persons developed an organized body that became known as the National Service Board for Religious Objectors (NSBRO). Above all expectation, they agreed to appoint an executive as secretary of this board to represent the movement in the city of Washington.

There were other organizations with the motive of peace in their charter. The International Fellowship of Reconciliation (IFOR) looked for fellowship with like-minded people. Besides representatives of the historic peace churches, Walter W. Van Kirk was elected to the board. He was executive secretary of the International Commission of Justice and Goodwill of the Federal Council of Churches of Christ in America and represented all member churches of the Federal Council. Some of the Protestant bodies, especially the Methodists and Disciples of Christ, were seeking a place in the fellowship of peace-minded Christians. Young people were taking a stand against war under the influence of the American Friends Service Committee (AFSC), the IFOR, and individuals like Sherwood Eddy and Kirby Page. Charles Boss of the Methodist Church and James H. Crain of the Disciples of Christ were appointed to represent conscientious objectors in churches other than historic peace churches.

The IFOR had been working for many years to cultivate peace and goodwill, both in and out of the churches, and had a long list of names of persons who had taken a stand against war. It was natural that A. J. Muste and Arthur Swift should find their way to the board of directors. Thus with seven agencies represented, there emerged a solid fellowship that carried through to the end of World War II. The persons involved had been working together in independent agencies, but now they united in a common cause, facing a difficult situation as they represented the young men who had taken a stand and needed a liaison between themselves and the government.

To keep the unity throughout the war period, the disciplines on the part of each group were voluntary. This became easier than any one anticipated. At the close of the war the cohesion lessened. The tendency was for the agencies to retreat to independence. However, the Church of the Brethren, having in the meantime formed the Brethren Service Commission (BSC), decided to search for next steps.

Leaders of the church were reluctant to accept freedom from participation in war without working actively for the development of peace through reconciliation and for the prevention of war. They felt that as soon as possible they should establish a relief program and call youth to represent the Church of the Brethren abroad and at home, as an alternative to war and to give a testimony of peace on behalf of the Church of the Brethren.

After its formation, the National Service Board had to find its way in representing conscientious objectors before the President of the United States, the Attorney General, and members of the Congress. Administrative contacts had to be established with the head of Selective Service. To do this, governmental agencies had to set up an arrangement whereby official encounters were made with the representatives of NSBRO, in behalf of all the churches and individuals involved.

Soon we were in the presence of General Lewis B. Hershey, the director of Selective Service. His staff was organized to implement the actions of Congress to provide alternative service. We faced many difficulties bringing together representatives from the churches and the government since the total situation was new for everyone. The individual draftee faced a new world alone. Administrators had to take responsibility alone. The NSBRO often had to act on behalf of constituent bodies without waiting for their official action. The detailed administration of the program of NSBRO with the government centered in two men, General Lewis B. Hershey for the government and Paul Comly French for the NSBRO.

Although the government would provide projects for alternative service to war, Selective Service would not allow conscientious objectors to go outside the United States. To find projects in places where the neighborhoods would agree to the presence of these young men was difficult. Gradually, opportunities came from many different localities for many types of work. Every project had to be studied with care, and always it had to be established through a person-to-person relationship rather than by some action of the community or the national government.

As we emphasized personal relationships in helping young men who were marked because of strong feelings against conscientious objectors, we discovered that young men and women could find their way to reconciliation through service anywhere in the world. The young draftee had to take his stand alone before the draft board. He had to leave his sheltered home and community and find himself with a restless group of men on a project of work that was not too exciting. His off-hours had limited opportunities for recreation. And in many places the young men were not welcome in the community. Yet as the years of the war passed these young men won a place with government agencies and churches so that, when the draft act was made permanent, freedom was granted to the conscientious objector to go anywhere in the world to serve. Let me emphasize that by personal encounter on the part of all involved there emerged a type of service heretofore not possible in wartime in the name of religion, and for Christian bodies in the name of Christ.

In this group of conscientious objectors there were representatives of 132 religious bodies along with persons who claimed no religion. The NSBRO made no distinction because of race, creed, or political belief. This fellowship, testing the ability of religious bodies to work together, created a basis for the faith that there could be cooperation in a program of relief and rehabilitation without losing identity of sponsoring bodies, and that the world was ready for a testimony of peace without war. The terrific current of this small group of people could not stop when the war was ended. It had to go on.

The Brethren administrators who were sent to places of need had to encounter people in authority of both church and state in order to make way for youth teams to enter in places where the Church of the Brethren was unknown. There were few people to make the introduction. Again, it was a situation of person-to-person encounter.

In the administration of these programs we followed advice learned in YMCA work in cantonments of the First World War. This was that in religious and recreational work we should always seek the highest person in authority for clearance. When this principle was observed and followed, doors opened. Brethren were on the spot to make good. To be granted a privilege and then to fail was unthinkable.

Presenting the hand of love often meant the shedding of tears. At times of reconciliation when there was still tenseness, it seemed natural to weep together in what was a high and joyful experience. The world is made up of individuals. Persons slaughter other persons in war; an act of reconciliation demands a firm handshake in a vow for peace.

The first entree of the Church of the Brethren in Europe was through the international YMCA in the person of Dr. Tracy Strong, the general secretary of that organization. He opened the way for Brethren to serve prisoners of war in England, France, Belgium, Holland, Germany, and several other countries. The experience with the YMCA was rewarding in many ways and gave a new vision of the future for service. For the first time Brethren Service became known in European circles with a special peace and service program. When the prisoners were freed they took with them the memory of what the YMCA had done for them. They remembered also the personal service rendered to them by Brethren Service representatives. Literature of the YMCA, including a description of Brethren Service work, went all over the world. Prisoners took the message to every community where they settled to begin life again. Ex-prisoners often gave expression of thanks for service rendered in the interest of goodwill.

Tracy Strong attended many world conferences. Any time he saw a Brethren Service worker, he would ask him to sit with him, and he always introduced the Brethren Service worker to the creative men and women in the area. When the Brethren were considering where they should establish headquarters in Europe, Dr. Strong offered rooms in the international YMCA building in Geneva, Switzerland, where he had an office. His entire staff welcomed us. But BSC had to make a decision. We felt that since we represented the church, we should identify ourselves with the World Council of Churches (WCC) which in 1948 was in the process of formation.

Dr. Strong kept a close relationship with Brethren Service in every country where we served. This fellowship was maintained on a deep spiritual level even in retirement. Without this personal fellowship the Church of the Brethren would have been afraid to move out in so many different places.

Dr. Edwin C. Bell, representing the Baptists, was in Paris when we first met him. He was seeking ways and means to get into Czechoslovakia and to contact needy people in Europe, with a special concern for members of the Baptist church in their homes and as refugees. With his help we made entrance into various fields, cooperating in every way possible and joining in numerous meetings for consultation in attempting to measure the total need and to secure the necessary materials for relief and rehabilitation, and above all, to help unite the Christian churches in an effort for a testimony of love to people. Many of them might have lost faith if they had not received a hand of helpfulness or heard that there was something good somewhere in the world.

Dr. Bell had his headquarters in Zurich, Switzerland, and the Brethren had theirs at Geneva. Many times conferences were called for consultation and planning. In Geneva we met Dr. Paul Garber, formerly of Virginia. He had the assignment for Methodists in Europe and North Africa. Because these relationships came early, such contacts furnished the foundation of Brethren Service work in Europe before the completion of the organization of WCC.

When it became clear that the Church of the Brethren would identify itself through Brethren Service to the World

Council of Churches, it was natural to think of setting up head-quarters with the World Council, then in process of formation. Before this time three representatives had come to America to confer with churchmen in the United States. This meeting was held in New York City, at which time Dr. Marc Boegner of France, Dr. G. K. A. Bell, the Bishop of Chichester, England, and W. A. Visser 't Hooft, secretary of the World Council, were interviewed.

The churches in America were still debating whether or not they should give sanction to a world relief program. Some were hesitant to join in relief work, feeling that attention should be given rather to the missionary program of the churches. When the question was asked of Dr. Visser 't Hooft, "Is there need for material aid in Europe?" he replied, "Yes." The second question was, "What is needed?" His reply was, "Food, clothing, bedding, and bicycles for ministers." A third question was, "Where should it be sent?" He replied, "Send it to Dr. Boegner in Paris." Dr. Boegner provided an address, and shipments began to go through Brethren Service channels.

Upon arrival in Geneva as administrators, we cleared with Dr. Visser 't Hooft as to where our office should be in Europe. He replied, "Probably Geneva." Work began with the organization which later was known as Inter-Church Aid and Service to Refugees. The first administrator with whom we worked was Dr. J. Hutchinson Cockburn. He was followed by Dr. Robert Mackie, who had been a leader in the World Christian Student Federation. Many meetings were held in Geneva with WCC and also with the United Nations agency, the World Health Organization, always keeping in touch with the United States representative. These contacts with persons from all over the world created a world background in regard to human need that would have been impossible otherwise.

The earliest trip into Germany brought us to Stuttgart, to meet with Dr. Eugen Gerstenmaier of *Hilfswerk,* who outlined the needs of the people and gave an estimate of quantities of material aid for various categories. He pointed out to us that some of the greatest needs would be centered around Kassel and to the northwest from there. We visited Bethel, at Bielefeld, an institution with many thousands of people, which included an epileptic colony, homes for the mentally ill, a regular hospital, and a deaconess training school headed up by

Fritz von Bodelschwingh. Plans were set up to assist in bringing material aid to this most important center in Germany.

We also contacted Bishop Hans Lilje at Hannover. He was just out of prison and was wearing borrowed clothes. He was living in a hospital that had been scheduled to relieve human suffering for those who desired to reestablish the Christian church. He had a typewriter and a bicycle in need of repairs. When he was asked to prepare a statement to the church in America, one sentence stood out: "We need oatmeal." He also needed communion sets for the church, robes for the priests, food and clothing for all. The statement, "We need oatmeal," was a symbol of the hunger of the country. This statement helped to move the Brethren in America to action and Dr. Lilje cooperated with many programs.

Dr. Georg Traar, a superintendent of the Protestant church in Austria, was one of the first persons volunteering to work cooperatively with us in Europe. He advised the Brethren to share an office in the Protestant church building. As a result we worked out a plan of supplying material aid through the church. By his introduction we were welcomed all over Austria. He met with Brethren again and again, including a visit to headquarters at Elgin in the United States. He spoke many times in deep appreciation of the work which the Brethren did through the Protestant church in Austria.

Because of the location of our representative at Bremen, Germany, we soon came to know Pastor H. J. Diehl, a liaison representative between the German government and the voluntary agencies. Pastor Diehl, in cooperation with Eldon Burke, did everything possible to prevent the tearing down of a military installation *(Friedehorst)* and to make it an institution of the German church. Old ladies and young women were moved into barracks. Sewing machines were provided. A child feeding center was developed. A training place for deaconesses was established; a workshop was set up for metal work, woodwork, printing, photography, shoe repair, and other handicraft. Brethren Service arranged for the securing of incubators and a tractor; eggs and chickens were sent later.

One very unusual person was Herr Werner Lott. He was the twenty-first German officer to be captured by the British in 1939. For seven years he was a prisoner in Canada. Then he came in touch with Brethren workers in prison camps. When he was released he became a YMCA secretary in Germany. Through him we were introduced to many practical opportunities for service. He reported that the German people were keen observers of the personal lives of foreigners and were most impressed by those who practiced what they preached. Werner Lott faced many difficult problems in a program set up by the German people for persons they classified as "endangered youth."

Pastor Wilhelm Mensching, who had been a missionary in Africa and then returned to Germany, faced many dangerous situations as a pastor and a pacifist during Hitler's regime. In cooperation with the IFOR, after World War II he developed an international peace center on a former military campground. Called *Freundschaftsheim,* it was built according to the plan of a year-round work camp, with short-time conferences. It became well known not only in Germany but around the world. Many people came there for group study and received the inspiration of Pastor Mensching's life.

Dr. Heinz Renkewitz, a refugee in Western Germany, who had come from Moravian headquarters in Herrnhut and was one of their leading historians, arrived in Geneva, Switzerland. One morning he inquired if it were possible to borrow $20,000 to establish refugee Moravians on swampland near the boundary between Holland and Germany. The World Council advised him to interview BSC. In the conversation regarding the matter we discovered that he had written a dissertation on the work of E. C. Hochmann von Hochenau; it included a detailed story of the early development of the Church of the Brethren at Schwarzenau, Germany. Dr. Renkewitz became a member of the Central Committee of WCC and gave time to the study of ways and means to aid refugees on its behalf. Later he joined the staff of the Evangelical Academy, which was sponsored by Martin Niemöller, at Arnoldshain near Frankfurt. Dr. Renkewitz became one of our best interpreters in understanding the Moravian church, the German people, the war, and its results. He always expressed strong interest in working for peace and goodwill through the churches.

In Italy, at the top levels of the Waldensian Church we found Pastor Guido Comba, and we developed our program with him in finding the places of greatest need and recommending materials for the best work in rehabilitation. He assisted in bringing in heifers, food and clothing, and exchange students. At Carrara, Italy, we learned to know a very young woman who could not speak English but desired to go to college in the States. McPherson College in Kansas offered to accept her as a student. She found it difficult to make her way because she knew only the Italian language. She arrived and was much loved by the faculty and the student body. She returned to Carrara, not knowing what exactly to do. The representative of Brethren Service got in touch with the American embassy in Rome and found they needed a person qualified as she was. She was invited for an interview and was employed.

In the hungry days of Carrara a fine group of young people became acquainted with Brethren Service. A number of these, mostly men, came to work camps in Germany and Austria. Several of them attended two or three camps in succession. For over ten years these young people kept in touch with Brethren Service although BSC work in Italy was discontinued. This is a sample of what happened where the service program operated and where we had persons to administer the program and render personal service in hospitals, as assistants to pastors, and in other projects.

The person who stands out most prominently in the entry of Brethren Service in Greece, helping us find our place in society and maintaining it, is Dr. Hamilcar Alivisatos, a lay theologian. He had the responsibility of heading up the relief program of the churches and engineered the development of the Greek team at Ioannina and throughout all Greece. Dr. Alivisatos attended most of the ecumenical meetings of WCC. He made special efforts to find Greek personnel to join with the foreign staff in building the Greek team. He interpreted the results of our operations not only to the church people throughout Greece but also to WCC and was exceedingly helpful in persuading the Greek government to trust Brethren Service workers.

In every country to which Brethren Service came, we made a special effort to cooperate with the highest authority of the church and state. In every case the result was their genuine appreciation for the work of our young people. They discovered that young people were capable and willing to do things heretofore not considered possible in many countries.

2. Beachheads for Service

by M. R. Zigler

During and following the Second World War the Church of the Brethren spontaneously began to stockpile materials for relief and rehabilitation. The church heard the cries of distress across the world from men, women, and children who needed food, clothing, and a place to call home. Around the earth there was a circle of destruction beneath which millions of human bodies lay buried without religious rites. Human beings passed into eternity without the opportunity of being at peace with their neighbors. In wartime people often die with revenge in their hearts toward unknown persons who had been ordered to strike. To heal the wounds in the hearts of those who survived the war and to create friendship based on Christian love meant that something had to be shared. To keep alive the bodies that housed the souls of men, it became necessary to reestablish family life, to create local community activities for mutual help, and to restore the Christian church as a body of believers.

The time came when hungry and stunned people began to move from the ashes of incendiary bombings and rose up to walk again into the future. The will to live motivated the blind to find their way around in an unknown world; the maimed found substitutes for hands and feet; the diseased and ill sought remedies for their ailing bodies. Millions of people needed the basic elements of food, clothing, and shelter. The urgency for action centered in their basic need for something to eat, something to wear, and something to sleep upon. It was difficult for people in America to realize the total and the urgent needs. Assuming Christian responsibility for sharing came slowly.

The Church of the Brethren had had limited experience in service in relief and rehabilitation beyond congregational and denominational limits. During and following the Revolutionary War, a small group of Brethren at Germantown, Pennsylvania, shared generously their resources. They followed the example of the Brethren at Schwarzenau, Germany, when, as a society of Brethren, they took care of refugees and invited other refugees into their fellowship. Following the Civil War, members of the church had the responsibility of caring for the suffering and destitute in the wake of the armies. At that time one person was named by the church to receive funds and transfer them to authorized persons in the areas of suffering where there had been loss of property by fire and confiscation as well as heavy burdens of taxation. Following the First World War, the Church of the Brethren answered a special call to aid in what was designated as Armenian relief. The response to this call was generous. One person was appointed to represent the Church of the Brethren in administering the program in a cooperative venture of relief agencies.

Between the two world wars many tons of clothing and food were collected and distributed, for the most part, through AFSC. The Brethren furnished materials and some staff persons in this cooperative venture. At many points the Church of the Brethren joined with the Friends, but never felt the responsibility to evaluate definitively world needs and to implement an administrative, indigenous program that would bring Brethren identity.

An important event occurred when AFSC invited the Church of the Brethren and the Mennonites to cooperate in a program of service in Spain. This was in the year 1937. The invitation was accepted. A larger responsibility for administration followed. Four persons were selected; and, for the first time, the church felt a strong personal relationship to foreign relief and rehabilitation and accepted responsibility. Sending a team of persons created a new dimension beyond the experience of giving materials only. Following an agreed-upon procedure with the Friends, our workers were located on both sides of the battle line in Spain. When the war was over, one of the Brethren representatives remained in Madrid for a number of years, ministering to those in need, especially the refugees.

In 1937 the Brethren accepted another unusual opportunity to send a representative to the world conference of the Protestant churches at Oxford and Edinburgh, bringing together two very important movements in the churches regarding "Life and Work" and "Faith and Order." It was clear at this meeting that the world was approaching a serious and dangerous upheaval among the nations. There was a feeling of restlessness among Christians in areas where the Protestant churches had tremendous and potential influence. Together the churches made a pronouncement that war is sin; that situations might occur where the right decision could not be made, and that there could be only a choice between a greater and a lesser evil. Because the charter of the Church of the Brethren is based on the teachings of the New Testament, the Brethren representative identified himself with a small minority at the conference of "Life and Work." He had to try to discover some way of eliminating war as a way of settling disputes among mankind. The discussion at this conference centered on the relationship of church and state. The usual debate on this subject followed, and the usual formula was confirmed.

Following these two conferences, our Brethren delegates visited Norway, Sweden and Denmark, then entered Germany for a period of time, and later Austria, Italy, and France. Conferences held in England and Scotland gave opportunity to feel the tenseness of the international situation. Because of a lost visa, it was not possible to go into Spain, a plan which had been arranged earlier. This was not too essential, however, since Brethren workers were there, and others were going.

Anticipating a world military storm, people felt that the United States would participate in it directly or indirectly. Many of the young men of the First World War were not satisfied with the repetition of the method utilized to relieve human suffering at the end of that war. They wanted to give a strong testimony for Christian peace. Several times between 1918 and 1941, proposals were offered as to how the Church of the Brethren could promote peace, give testimony against war, and provide ways of preparation if war should ever occur again. The Brethren developed an image of the Church of the Brethren as it ought to be, and planned ways and means whereby young people would be able to dedicate themselves to the ways of peace, hoping the church at large would support the program. The experience in Spain was a realistic maneuver that prepared the way for the church to do something alone as well as to cooperate with others equally at administrative planning tables.

With the experience of Civilian Public Service (CPS) during wartime, and especially in the establishment of an agreement with the government for a training unit to go to a foreign country, namely China, a special training unit was set up at Manchester College, North Manchester, Indiana. Men were selected for the unit, and were as far as South Africa on their way to China when the Congress decided that no funds could be used outside the United States for conscientious objectors. This disappointment gave pause to the relief movement. There was need for patience, further study, and waiting for the appropriate time.

Finally, in 1946, under the organization of the United Nations Relief and Rehabilitation Administration (UNRRA), we were able to send sixty young men to China to teach farmers how to use tractors as a means of producing food for the Chinese people. With the tractor unit were several who spent time in administrative tasks under the direction of Harlan Cleveland, the head of the United Nations organization in China, and specifically under the direction of William Green, the head of the division of food and agriculture. Persons involved in this experience were scattered all over China, north, east, south, and west.

It should be recorded also that the Brethren had experience in providing services for the rebuilding of war and famine areas on the mission fields of India and China and left a record of using excellent methods and unusual achievements. These incidents, however, were limited to the fields which provided a backlog of experience in making preparations and creating plans to enter the European war zone.

About the year 1940 the international YMCA invited the Church of the Brethren to participate in the program it had developed on behalf of the prisoners of war located in England, Canada, and parts of Europe. Musical instruments were provided for the Canadian camps. One prisoner near Lake Louise, Canada, a prisoner for almost a decade, reported that the first time he saw the name Brethren was on a musical instrument in the prison camp, but he did not meet a representative of the Church of the Brethren until he returned to Germany. There he met four Brethren who served in the YMCA prisoner-of-war work in England, Belgium, and Germany.

This program made the church aware of the large number of war prisoners and their needs. After the prisoners were released and placed in their homes and communities in Germany, they formed a constituency of people who knew of the Church of the Brethren in a country where the church had not been known. The program consisted of educational projects designed to meet the needs of the individual prisoner, and preparation for his return to civilian life. A recreational program was provided for the health and welfare of the men in camp. A religious program was offered not only for their immediate needs but also to prepare leadership for the churches that had to be rebuilt when they returned to their home communities.

The historic peace churches, consisting of the Society of Friends, the Mennonites, and the Church of the Brethren, found a mutual and natural fellowship in giving a testimony for peace and service. Each maintained its own identity, but there was a feeling of oneness as they moved in parallel lines, both in the securing of funds and materials and in the distribution of these in areas of need. AFSC, the Mennonite Central Committee (MCC), and BSC were each keenly aware of the common objectives and the need for a service program as an initial step in the building of a creative peace, with the hope that there would never be another world war. The three historic peace churches joined with other relief agencies in the international voluntary service organization and were registered as relief agencies and ready for operation in foreign countries.

AFSC had, since its beginning, developed a magnificent program that was recognized internationally when it received the Nobel peace prize (1947). Many churches of various denominations and individuals supported the program because they trusted its administration and were satisfied with the service rendered. The people who received help from the Friends responded. The Friends enjoyed a worldwide fellowship. Because of their many years of experience they had administrators ready for the task.

The Mennonites, because of their own suffering in scattered parts of the world, had an experience of securing support and providing for a ministry to their own people in many lands. Their program of service covered many years of Mennonite history. After the First World War a large group of Mennonite men were sent abroad to administer a program of relief and rehabilitation. When the doors were opened to enter military areas to help refugees and to reestablish homes, churches, and communities, the Mennonites were ready.

The youngest of the three historic peace churches, the Church of the Brethren, being an American church without members in the war area of Europe, and not having much experience in administration, found some difficulty in matching the skills of the other groups in securing qualified persons and resources. The Friends and the Mennonites shared their experiences and in many ways provided the Brethren with insights and helpful suggestions. BSC was eventually able to carry its share of the load in the ministry of peace, service, and goodwill.

When the way was clear, the Friends, Mennonites, and Brethren found their way through Warsaw up to the border of Russia. They were together in the flooded areas of the Yellow River in China. Their personnel went into Italy and other countries of Europe, working together as a unit or separately in the same country. The task on the field was stupendous. Every agency knew that even working together we could not do all that needed to be done. Always there was a challenge for each to serve in a larger way and to do more to occupy neglected areas. A comradeship was developed in every country among those who sought to relieve human suffering.

Virtually every church in Europe had its counterpart in the relief agencies. The Catholics could invite the Catholic group known as *Caritas;* the Jewish people could invite the American Joint Distribution Committee; the Lutherans, the Lutheran World Federation; the Unitarians, the Unitarian Service Committee. The Friends and the Mennonites both had strong constituencies that could give extraordinary invitation and welcome and therefore were recognized by the various governments. But Brethren Service had no such constituency. For the Brethren to be ready to serve it was necessary to have an understanding with the state. The only way to be recognized on entering a foreign country was to approach the highest authority of the government and the churches. Permission was needed for administrators to be allowed to travel freely and to make custom clearance possible.

It is one thing to register officially with church and state, but it is something more to "register your presence" among the people in a personal way. A sharing testimony must be provided in such a way that there will be no doubt about the sincerity of persons promoting the message of peace. It was not an easy thing to establish confidence among those desperately in need of the essentials of everyday living, especially in a territory where just a few months earlier Americans had been known as enemies, and now they were on the scene to offer needed resources.

The first real personal contact with those made destitute by the war was through the YMCA in its program of war prisoner aid. This trail of service, covering a period of six years, records the experience of four Brethren Service workers employed by the World's Alliance of the YMCA. One of the essential aspects of the program was to quicken the religious life among prisoners and to restore a faith which had been blasted by national socialism or by total war. Workers sought to prepare men to return to Germany and other countries for Christian service. In Norton camp in England they organized a complete theological seminary in which the faculty and students were all prisoners. Refresher courses were arranged for approximately 150 pastors who had been in service. At this time there were 400,000 men in the camps. Books and periodicals of a definite religious nature were produced in the camps. The Church of the Brethren furnished 2,000 German Bibles to be used there. For educational purposes, millions of books went into the prison camps of Europe, and tens of thousands of classes were held on all manner of subjects preparing men for the future.

The YMCA cooperated with religious and other welfare organizations in this ministry. On a worldwide basis, the YMCA offered a lay approach to the ecumenical church. This provided a way for all relief agencies of a religious nature to join in a combined service—including the Roman Catholics—in preparing prisoners of war to return to their homes.

Brethren representatives urged that opportunities should be provided for prisoners to participate in their own rehabilitation. These men should be helped to rebuild their personalities and develop a sense of responsibility. Therefore, a large part of the prisoner-of-war work in England was put on a self-supporting basis. By providing means of earning resources, 100,000 men were able to pay from their small salaries $1.20 per week for educational films. Two million German books published in England more than paid for themselves. Articles ranging from footballs to violins were purchased by prisoners at reasonable prices. In Belgium the prisoners themselves paid for some 150,000 food packages for their needy families in Germany. About 50,000 textile parcels were sent. Brethren Service provided about $7,000 worth of food, clothing, shoes, and soap for the returning prisoners from Russia. The only things they had been able to bring with them were the tattered clothing on their backs, a mess kit, and unpleasant memories.

A special guideline was set up for the prisoner-of-war work in 1947: to emphasize the importance of the individual and to gird this individual with the armor of faith. To accomplish these goals the religious program needed to be intensified. The information service and educational planning were designed to help the individual to become a self-respecting man without being exploited.

The policy of the international YMCA was to minimize its own vigorous activities and to stress the indigenous organizations of the different countries to which the prisoners would return. Finally, the representatives of the Church of the Brethren also found their way to other tasks. The church finished its relationship with the YMCA, regretting the break in fellowship and comradeship but enjoying the satisfaction of the experience in cooperation.

The first European country opened to the Church of the Brethren for relief work following World War II was France. The establishment of the Brethren Service program came about through the agreements made by the American Aid for France on the stateside, and the American Aid for France in France. On the stateside, there was a French woman as executive, and on the French side the executive secretary was Dr. George W. Bakeman of the Medical College of Virginia. France had suffered the invasion of the Germans and also the coming of the Allies at the end of the war. The description of a small village prepared by the mayor of Jeanmenil on October 16, 1945, presents a typical situation in the war-torn areas of France. Multiplied on a national scale, the picture brought a mass challenge to provide food, clothing, and shelter in every way possible.

Jeanmenil, a village of the Vosges region, had 690 inhabitants. Of these 684 had suffered some injuries, 310 lost their entire possessions, and 374 lost most of their possessions. The village no longer had a church nor a parsonage nor a place for men to work. A school for girls had been destroyed. The electrical conduit was cut in twenty-four places, and all electrical lines slashed. Of eighty-one houses sixty were destroyed; twenty-one were damaged but reparable; only five were habitable. Farmhouses were burned or damaged by shells or made roofless and doorless. There were no cattle, no tools, no linens.

Likewise in the city of Jeanmenil, during the siege of October, the inhabitants were living in caves, closed in, and forbidden to leave. They were without bread or water, fire or light. The village was bombarded without respite. The houses flamed one after another. Finally the inhabitants were ordered to leave at six in the evening, all of them—women with new babies, the aged, the sick, the paralytic. They were ordered to go into the unknown, leaving behind their clothing, their tools, their kitchenware—all that they could not carry with them.

In the canton of Senones all men between the ages of eighteen and sixty were deported. Of the 950 people who were placed in torture camps at Stutthof, Dachau, Buchenwald, 650 died of torture, starvation, or in the gas chambers. Left in the canton were 450 widows, 700 orphans, and others dependent on the missing men and in the greatest need. Out of 950 deportees only 294 returned, and they were in no condition to work. Most of them had tuberculosis.

To answer this need 122 bales of clothing were sent to Moussey in the Senones Valley, 30 bales to Jeanmenil, 27 bales to Le Tholy, making a total of 179 bales. These made "many, many people happy."

In 1946 two representatives were assigned to Dunkirk in cooperation with American Relief for France, and in 1947 they reported that they had distributed milk to 17,000 children in that area. Medical milk, baby cereals, and children's clothing were supplied to dispensaries and health centers for children and to the French Red Cross. Children in vacation colonies and summer camps were supplied with orange juice, milk, chocolate powder, rice, jam, sugar, and lentils.

From the Church of the Brethren had come 960 bales of clothing and blankets, kitchen utensils, toys, and shoes, which were distributed to 35,000 people. Five pastors received bicycles. In the community center ironing and sewing facilities were set up, English lessons were taught, and reading and recreational activities provided. Summer holiday camps were established for children, providing 4,910 with milk, chocolate, orange juice, jam, sugar, soups, and cereals. Workers secured materials for the tuberculosis sanitarium, and in cooperation with the normal agencies of the community they helped refugees and disabled people find their way back to their homes.

Another very important method whereby the Church of the Brethren aided in France was through a shipment of 150 heifers in September, 1945. These were distributed in six *Départements* (states). The original idea was to ship 150 head of cattle to the Spanish government to follow the program of 1937 in Spain. But Spain, at this time, could not receive the gift, and an offer was made to the French government through Paul B. Anderson, chairman of the American Council of Voluntary Agencies for Foreign Service. The director of economic affairs of the French department of agriculture accepted the offer that the cows of different breeds would be distributed according to the season.

The administration of relief work is seldom easy. It is difficult to secure materials on a voluntary basis to meet specific needs. It is difficult also to create a common mind on the part of responsible officials, both those with resources to share and those representing the recipients. The arguments against the heifer project were: (1) too much shipping space was required; (2) American livestock might bring in disease; (3) there was better economy in canned milk and meats; (4) the milk shortage was due to lack of feed and transport, not cattle.

On October 16, 1945, in the Orien newspaper there was the announcement, "Fifteen days ago the Liberty ship *Zona Gale* brought to Le Havre 160 horses, 150 milk cows, and 75 tractors from America."

Fourteen Brethren farmers came from Pennsylvania and Ohio with the shipment of cows to take care of them on the boat. Accompanied by M. Sauger, director of the Agricultural Service of the Lower Seine, they visited the Preventorium of Canteleu, the institution of Grugny, and the farms of Octeville, and Fontaine and La Lett—places where some of the cows were located. The farmer visitors were called "seagoing cowboys." One of them was able to identify the cow he had personally given.

The assistance rendered by BSC was recognized by the government and the churches of France, both Catholic and Protestant. Our workers at Dunkirk and in administration in Paris were presented with special honors for service given in the name of the Church of the Brethren in France.

For a while Brussels, Belgium, became the center of Church of the Brethren activity both in prisoner work and in the initiation of the material aid program. From this center exploratory trips were made into Germany. One shipment of heifers was distributed to farmers, and many tons of food and clothing given to people who needed them. Eldon R. Burke, director, described the reception of Brethren Service material:

"It is between seasons in Belgium. The new potatoes are not yet on the markets. The old ones are extremely scarce. There are six Protestant-supported institutions in Brussels, all in need of supplies and money. Let me give you a glimpse of the recipients of food. On Saturday, June 22, Pastor Paul DeWilde, a YMCA secretary and a local Protestant minister, took me by jeep with a load of beans and rice. We went first to an orphanage *Orphelinat Protestant,* supported by the Belgium missionary church.... We went on to the *Maison des Enfants,* supported by the Methodist mission in which there were thirty-four children. They had no potatoes at all, and the manager of the home said, 'I haven't seen beans for years.' ... The third stop was at *Paix du Soir,* an old people's home supported by the Silo mission where there were twenty-nine persons. There we left two bags of rice and one of beans.

"The next place was *Refugée Protestant,* an old folks' home with thirty occupants, operated by the Union of Churches. The *Clinique Protestant,* a twenty-five-bed hospital, owned by the Union of Churches, was seriously in need of rice. Here was an interesting discovery, that I was from BSC. They knew the name immediately, and then said they were very grateful for the sheets, pillow cases, and towels which they had already received, bearing Brethren Service labels, which made it possible for them to use more beds. The clinic had been damaged by a flying bomb.

"The last stop on this distribution day was Mother's Home, a home for unmarried mothers. One of the nurses told us that they had just gotten to the place where they were going to have to buy potatoes on the black market. On the following Thursday we took food to the summer camp at Lustin near Laumer, a camp operated by the Belgian YMCA. What a thrill it was to see that this small shipment of Brethren food got to the places where it was much needed and appreciated. One of the recipients wrote a letter as follows: 'You have been good enough to send the precious food for our inmates. I want to send you the heartiest thanks for the *Comité de Paix* (peace committee).'"

Pastor William G. Thonger of the Council of the Federation of Protestant Churches wrote, "Will you allow me to seize this opportunity for asking you to convey to all concerned the expression of our warmest gratitude for all that has been done to help our Belgian Protestantism in the spirit of need and opportunity? I have been in a good position to appreciate the remarkable generosity and competence of this outstanding service."

As early as June, 1945, Margaret Watson of the YMCA made an official exploratory survey of Holland with special reference to children's centers. Immediately the distribution of material aid was started for children's camps. Also, there were displaced centers which housed Dutch people to be repatriated; Dutch men who had married German women, being held until they were to be sent to Germany; people of Dutch origin who had been living in Germany; stateless people of all kinds, including a group of Dutch Mennonites who had lived for generations in Russia; and children of collaborators whose mothers and fathers were being held in prisons. These centers were housed in labor camps, old factory and school buildings, and monasteries.

We tried to find homes for the orphan children and to help those who were released from prison. The size of the camps ranged from twenty to four hundred persons. In some centers there was good organization of materials, and in others there was need for materials. Clothing of all types was urgently needed. It was unusual for a camp to have sheets for beds. We sought to help eliminate the camps by placing every resident in some home or new situation. The purposes of Brethren Service work in Holland were summarized as follows: "At the moment ... it is supporting the work of the World's Alliance of the

YMCA with its project for the children who have been made orphans through the war or as a result of the conflict. We hope later to supply additional material for this project in order to not only enlarge the scope of the World Alliance's activities, but to add to it a material relief program."

In October, 1944, the dykes on Walcheren Island were bombed in four places by the Allies to force evacuation of the Germans. The city of Flushing was bombed many times. Except for a few thousand people who were evacuated to Zeeland, the residents of Flushing suffered indescribable losses. Thirty-six thousand shells fell on Flushing, and in two and one-half hours the British were able to land and to capture a small section of the city. By November 3 the town was captured, and in a few more days the British possessed the entire island.

After the bombardment only one house remained undamaged in the city of Flushing. For the reestablishment of the island, "gaps in the dykes more than a mile in length were tackled with an indescribable passion which throughout the ages has enabled the Dutch, and especially the Zeelanders, to get the better end of the struggle against wind and water. Because of storms on the sea, much of the work was destroyed again and again, but finally the dykes were repaired and the people began to return to their homes. Instead of feeling bitter, they seemed happy to be free to start again." Brethren Service undertook a material aid project on the island.

A committee was established in the United States to work in behalf of the people in Holland, and an organization set up in Holland to receive and distribute materials. Brethren personnel remained in Holland until most of the material aid had been distributed and the doors were beginning to open to enter Germany. We felt that the people of Holland were organizing themselves and were able to receive and distribute their gifts without personnel from other countries assisting. Special recognition was granted by the government, and messages of appreciation were received by BSC for the arrival of materials and persons to help in the rehabilitation program in Holland.

Our experience in France, Belgium, and Holland revealed that the greatest difficulty was to be able to evaluate the needs, to request material, and to have it arrive at the opportune time and season of the year. Especially was this true in regard to agricultural interests and the type of clothing needed. There were many delays in shipment and in custom clearance procedures. At times materials would come quickly and at the right time, but often transportation facilities were unavailable. Therefore we purchased trucks and employed truck drivers as quickly as possible to guarantee efficient distribution.

All relief agencies anticipated entering Germany at the earliest possible moment, but first the military governments must grant permits. Nearly all agencies were organizing missions to Germany and collecting materials for distribution. An organization of relief agencies was established to unite the work into one operation in which all would act independently but would eliminate overlapping and guarantee aid to all the needy. This organization in Germany and the United States was called Council of Relief Agencies Licensed for Operation in Germany (CRALOG). It was a permanent mission and served as a liaison between the military governments, the German indigenous agencies, and the American voluntary agencies.

Eleven organizations were selected to go to Germany. These were: AFSC, BSC, Committee on Christian Science Wartime Activities of The Mother Church, Church Committee on Overseas Relief and Reconstruction of the Federal Council of Churches in Christ, International Rescue and Relief Committee, Labor League for Human Rights of the American Federation of Labor, Lutheran World Relief, MCC, Community Service Committee of the Congress of Industrial Organizations, Unitarian Service Committee, and Catholic Relief Services.

In order to measure the total need in Germany annual meetings were held to estimate how to develop a unified program, with each agency administering its own program. There was no referee or any one person who was the guiding spirit, but guidelines were worked out for operations. Generally each agency was assigned a specific task in certain areas, and in the largest and most needy fields all agencies were organized to cover the field. The representative of the Church of the Brethren, Eldon R. Burke, after some time had elapsed became the executive chairman. He was located at Bremen and represented CRALOG in the receiving of materials from abroad and dispersing them to the proper agencies as designated by CRALOG stateside. This was a difficult and delicate task, but through experience CRALOG developed methods that were satisfactory to the various agencies and to the German people.

Before the Brethren Service representatives moved in for their own program of material aid, they had been working in the international YMCA assignments with prisoners of war. Through this activity, they were able to forecast the needs and study the locations of operations. It was soon evident that there were many places where Brethren Service had opportunities. Refugees on the road indicated that there was need for housing and locating displaced persons. The millions of refugees coming from the East joined the people who had been driven from their homes in Western Germany and were returning, many of them only to see the rubble of their own homes and the graves of their loved ones. Few of the cities had good water supplies, and heating facilities were broken. Food production and its distribution had not been organized. Everything seemed to be in chaos. Because of limited resources and personnel, it was necessary to select a few things to do for the German people.

The division of Germany into military zones, American, British, French, and Russian, made the work more difficult than if the country had a unified government. The churches of Germany tried to maintain a unified administration across all borders. However, it was impossible for the German people to ignore the zonal requirements.

Soon the German government was reorganized in harmony with the decision of the military occupation authorities, and facilities were inaugurated relating CRALOG to the German welfare agency, so that German people and the welfare agencies could mutually help distribute materials in every part of occupied Germany. Brethren workers served in Stuttgart in the interest of the YMCA youth movement and to help with the distribution of materials. Others were assigned to Frankfurt to offer heifers for distribution by agricultural agencies, to work out plans for work camps, and to develop a program of exchange so that German youth could go to America and Americans to Germany.

It soon became clear that Berlin would not be the center of activity for the Brethren. It became necessary, therefore, to find a place where the Brethren might establish an operational center for material aid and an office of administration in relationship to exchange students, refugees, and the heifer project. As Schwarzenau was the birthplace of the Brethren, this drew attention to Kassel, located in the central part of Germany. It was almost totally a destroyed city, about sixty miles from Schwarzenau. It was only a short distance from Marburg and Hannover and within twenty-nine miles of the east-west border. It was directly east of Cologne at the juncture of the three zones, American, British, and Russian. Kassel was found to be predominantly Protestant. It had been neglected. The city had good railroad facilities, and the *Autobahn* was nearby. Brethren Service seemed to be welcomed in the city both by military personnel and the city administration.

So we decided that the operational program in the European theater would center in Kassel, Germany, rather than in Geneva, Switzerland. There was a feeling of solidarity and strength. The city gave us land in a park area in which to build a center in the name of the Church of the Brethren. So Kassel became the beachhead for the Brethren in Germany.

After studying a European map and reading reports of the needs in Austria, we concluded that the Church of the Brethren should give special attention to Austria. It was a small nation and might be more easily served by the Brethren than a larger country. As quickly as Austria was ready to work with outside agencies, Ralph Smeltzer went directly to Vienna to offer the BSC material aid program, including in a special way the heifer project. General Mark Clark was commander of the United States Forces in Austria. On October 24, 1946, he made a broadcast appeal, stating that the food situation in Austria "now approximates starvation diet." He pointed out that UN-RRA had been unable to increase the 1200 calories of the Austrians; the German diet had been increased to 1500 calories. Therefore it was a challenge to the Brethren to aid in whatever way possible to increase the food supply. The general also appealed for shoe manufacturers to send contributions so that 18,000 Austrian children would not have frozen feet the following winter.

Brethren Service, feeling that there should be a center of operations, upon the advice of General Clark selected Linz, a city that was destined to receive much of the refugee population. In cooperation with the Austrian church and the Austrian government, we surveyed the needs of the Austrian people and developed a plan to distribute the usual materials for survival.

Special attention was given to the agricultural aspects for the purposes of rehabilitation. We distributed heifers to farmers, goats for families in the villages, seeds for gardens and fields, chickens and turkeys for all. The administrative headquarters was centered primarily in Vienna and operational affairs at Linz.

From the very beginning of our work in Austria we maintained a close association with the reconstruction committee of the Protestant churches of Austria and of Church World Service/World Council of Churches (CWS/WCC). Since Austria was not completely divided politically like Germany, it was easier to create a program in cooperation with the national agencies of the country. There was not the difficulty of meeting requirements of several divisions, although there were established military occupational zones. Personnel was needed for the interests of health, education, recreation, and agriculture. In cooperation with the Austrian people, we secured trucks and distributed materials throughout the nation.

Through UNRRA we were able to enter Poland with a shipment of heifers. The shipment came from Baltimore on a Liberty ship, the *Santiago Iglesias,* with Holstein and Guernsey cattle. The Brethren had donated 150 heifers. On the ship, the heifers were attended by eight Brethren, eight Mennonites, one Methodist, and one Roman Catholic. Workers were permitted to enter Poland, and soon there were seven resident representatives. Headquarters had to be located in Warsaw, but most of the distributions were in Ostroda. The work really began in December, 1946. Progress was very slow because of problems of location, housing, competent interpreters, and transportation. As fast as possible, clothing, and medical supplies were distributed, and seeds of all kinds provided for the gardens and fields. By August, 1947, 727 heifers had been given to Poland. We launched projects of sewing, shoe repairing, and small home industries. One of the most appreciated gifts was one hundred sets of harness delivered to farmers. A purebred Percheron stallion was presented to Warsaw Agricultural College. In this manner Brethren Service went to work in Poland in one of the most devastated of the cities.

AFSC invited BSC to join in a relief and rehabilitation program in Italy. In Italy, as in all other suffering nations, there were men, women, and children needing food, clothing, and shelter. Because of the low income of many people before the war, followed by the results of war, it was impossible for an observer to evaluate the total need of body, mind, and soul, as the struggle went on to reestablish family life and a helpful civil and church fellowship. The reorientation from a dictatorship to a democratic society, after the terrifying events of the war, demanded courage and faith to overcome the hopelessness featured in every face of the population. There was no other way to forecast the immediate future. The farmers had lost their tools and animals and their manpower. Women and children, the old men and those back from the army, many of whom were sick or crippled, took the lead in planting seeds in the fields and flowers in the rubble. They began to sing again. There was evidence that the opera would come back.

The Italian government and the churches, both Catholic and Protestant, welcomed the gifts that came through UNRRA and all other relief agencies. As usual, the Brethren offered material aid—food, clothing, soap, sewing machines, bedding, and an unusually large number of heifers. Representatives of the Italian government kept a careful record of the animals received, and of the gifts of female calves given to other farmers. If for reason of disease or sickness an animal had to be slaughtered, the record stated the reason. The government authorized the management through the agency of a cooperative.

One of the most unusual things about the Italian service program was the fact that we sent young married couples without children, most of them seminarians. As the United Nations retired from the field, the work was turned over to the Italians.

The Brethren who had been scattered over Italy concentrated on Carrara. This was one of the towns that had not been too extensively damaged during the war, although the battle line for many months was only a few miles south of the town. While Carrara itself lost only a few buildings during the war, its hinterland suffered severely. The people coming in from the country, away from the war area, created a crowded population problem in the small city. Within fifteen days after UNRRA closed its program a club known as "OK" was started.

Why was Carrara selected? A report described conditions there in these words: "Carrara's children are seasoned war veterans. They saw the Germans come and leave. They saw the Americans (Filipinos they called them, since the liberation troops were Japanese-American) come and go. They watched the partisans during the war as well as after. Many of them spent some of the coldest winter months in the marble quarries to escape gunfire. Some of them saw their loved ones killed as they walked the streets. Others heard a large building being converted into a monument of bricks and stone as our own bombers buried more than a hundred women and children in its rubble. These pictures have made lasting impressions upon the minds and bodies of Marco, Renato, Mariella, and more than 300 other Carrara children now in the club of the *Americani.* It is our desire to soften the hardened tissue of these scars of war in the community."

Promised shipments of materials to European countries generally preceded the coming of personnel. The words "Brethren Service" were becoming familiar because they were seen on boxes and cartons containing gifts from churches and friends in America. The coming of people to help in the administration of distribution was a designed feature of Brethren Service so that there might be a fellowship handshake to express the ultimate message of the Church of the Brethren in the name of Christ for peace on earth and goodwill to men. Even though the first encounter created an expression of joy and achievement and reconciliation on the part of the giver of the gift and the person receiving the gift, it was not enough to create confidence because neither could anticipate how one representing a conquering nation and the other a conquered nation would react after the first handclasp.

The beachheads were well chosen. The reception on the part of the people was very warm. But several years of intimate fellowship in a community were required before the words, "We trust you," could be distinctly heard in the community. In all fairness, it must be said that it generally took several years for an individual representative of the Church of the Brethren to trust those who heretofore were enemies. Reconciliation was highly desirable, but most difficult to establish in the presence of mass cemeteries. The records of Dachau and Buchenwald, the destroyed cities and villages, church spires with sanctuaries missing, smokestacks of industry standing in rubble and ashes, men with parts of their bodies injured, many blind, widows and children homeless, worn-out farm animals and equipment, lack of fire to heat the rooms crowded with people, not enough food to go around, scanty clothing, an old piece of rag for a dishcloth—these were European realities.

The ever-present, annoying question that plagued every representative of the conquering nations was how to be a humble, sincere, equal-basis partner in reconciliation and in sharing gifts of love. Reconciliation often took place in silence. There were no words in the language to express the anguish of those served, or the humiliation of these who had come out of a land of abundance into a devastated land. This extraordinarily difficult feat had to be accomplished person to person and face to face. It was not easy for needy people to receive the gifts. They were unable to pay for them or work for them. It was not until the sincerity of the giver was transparent that Christian reconciliation took place. A new fellowship developed out of the memories of both conquering and conquered spirits, something like a beautiful sunrise after a dark night of fear.

3. The Confluence of Living Streams

by M. R. Zigler

After World War II there were many streams of influence flowing in and out in the restless population of mankind. In order to survive, scattered people with different languages had to find ways and means to rebuild families, communities, and nations. Each stream, having its own characteristics, demanded compromises of all sorts and understandings from differences, so there could be some common fellowship in reestablishing the essentials of living. Naturally, people found their way to national groups, and within the national groups they found language groups and religious fellowships. The cohesion of so many people from different countries in a new order centered around the most universal objective—to rebuild communities.

Besides the coming together of nationals, there were other streams of influence that had to be recognized. Likely the strongest influences were the military powers. Every nation had its military concept and its implementations. The conquering nations faced difficulties as did the conquered. The whole economic order had to be revamped from a vigorous wartime schedule to the task of rebuilding industry, establishing new farm production quotas, arranging the return of personnel from the armed forces, and rebuilding the world so that people everywhere might have food, clothing, and shelter, and that there might be peace in the future.

Every encounter of one culture with another, whatever the factors involved, can be compared to the coming together of two rivers in what is known as "confluence." Each of the flowing streams loses identity in a way, and in fact a new river is formed. In the physical world the laws of God operate easily in creating a new river by two others flowing together. One stream coming in may be filled with glacier deposits; the other coming out of a clear lake could provide abundance of clear water. The combined waters of two rivers join and the water clears again. As living streams of humanity from different sources form a confluence, differences in language, customs, manners, aims, and architecture, as well as differing methods in administration and ways of farming create a rugged situation.

In the period following the war there was need for a speedy and common agreement on ways of rebuilding society in all its aspects. There were many different streams of thinking among those who used the same language—theologians, the military, businessmen, educators, farmers, scientists. In normal times professional people often live and move among those of the same profession; likewise, in the economic area. Worshipers find their way to the church of their faith. But these were not normal times. The fundamentals of providing food and clothing and shelter had to be agreed on. The essentials of language had to be learned as rapidly as possible.

We who came as visitors and strangers found it necessary to understand the habits and background of individuals. By experience and training we had to decide such simple matters as when to shake hands or when to dress formally. We must make sure not to offend by failing to observe the customs and manners of others. This was especially true in church and state affairs. We needed a growing awareness of the desire of others to understand and to be understood.

Through its service program, the Church of the Brethren found its way into a mass of conflicting streams seeking to form a new stream in society. We came with resources of persons and materials designed to purify as far as possible the stream that was filled with hatred, revenge, and hopelessness. It was clear that the church would not be able, because of limited resources, to provide a highly trained administrative force. All we could do was to send young men and women who would serve on a sacrificial basis for a two-year period of time at $7.50 per month and maintenance. We needed a minimum number of administrators who could organize the youth to take care of distributing heifers to refugee farmers, getting food and clothing to the needy directly and through other agencies, and helping in refugee camps, hospitals, and other community agencies. A large number of men, none of them specialists, under a competent builder operated successfully as carpenters in a way that the Europeans could not understand. Others worked with youth on the farm, building artificial insemination centers and helping farmers understand the new methods used in their home farms in the States. Thousands of men, known as seagoing cowboys, helped to transport animals from the United States to many nations.

Beyond the normal problems there were others arising out of military controls. These were apparent in every nation. In the early stages of rebuilding the European commonwealth it was difficult to associate with the nationals because there were orders against fraternization, particularly in Germany. Gradually these controls were lifted, and representatives could work together. Finally, Brethren volunteers were permitted to enter German homes, as well as the homes of other nationals. Naturally this freedom made it possible for marriage to take place between Brethren Service workers and nationals of the countries being served.

One staff member and his wife called from their home in Indiana to offer their service as team leaders in Greece. One day in an orphanage there they saw a beautiful child. They were attracted to her and wanted to adopt her. According to the rules of adoption, they were able to bring her to America as their daughter.

The names and addresses of the givers of food packages offered a contact whereby family-to-family correspondence was established in many cases. Bremen, Indiana, and Bremen, Germany, formed a twin city fellowship. A representative from Bremen, Indiana, visited Bremen, Germany, and an exchange student from Germany spent a year in a home in Indiana.

The German church went all out in expressing appreciation for the gifts of material aid in the hard years of 1946 and 1947. Its leaders were amazed that a nation could pour tons of food and clothing into a conquered nation so quickly after the fighting ceased.

Many streams coming from many directions eventually formed one great river of human development. The old regime was gone. The church had changed. Governmental controls had broken down. With whirling masses of people, unable to communicate with one another for one reason or another, there was a division in every country in politics. Several political ideologies aimed for the loyalty and commitment of every citizen, challenging each to become a follower either of democracy or communism. Barriers of language, habits, customs, manners, and methods of administration were cleared away to make possible a decision between two political movements of worldwide significance.

It was not possible to measure the great massive rivers of influence, but smaller streams became significant. Schwarzenau in Germany, the birthplace of the Church of the Brethren, represented one stream of influence. Here visitors came who would speak for the Church of the Brethren. Here meetings would be held in the interest of the Church of the Brethren. Something should be visible here, we thought, to indicate that this is the place that marks the beginning of the Church of the Brethren. The school building in the village had long been in need of repair and improvement, and when the refugees came in, it was overcrowded. We called for funds to reconstruct the school building. Resources were made available. A new building was erected. Over the water fountain in the building are the words: "Alexander Mack School, in honor of the eight founders of the Church of the Brethren under the leadership of Alexander Mack, Schwarzenau/Eder, 1708. The Church of the Brethren on September 4, 1955, presented a generous gift for the education of the children of the Schwarzenau community in the spirit of peace and good will among men."

As an unexpected result of the exchange of thousands of European youth in American homes and American youth in European homes, many American parents made special trips to Europe to visit those they had entertained in their homes. Young people from American homes entered into volunteer service, many of them going to areas from which exchange students had come. A number of American pastors served with pastors in Germany, and ministers from European churches came to America to serve for a brief time in American churches.

One of the most fertile streams of influence was the resettlement of refugees in America. A special staff of workers served in Austria and in Germany and on the stateside to assist both the refugees and the sponsoring families. A transaction, requiring faith both on the part of the refugee and the American family had to be agreed upon before the refugee could be given a visa to enter the United States.

Another effective encounter between Americans and Europeans was that of the seagoing cowboys who helped take shipments of heifers to their destination in Europe. They often followed through to contact the European family selected by the government to receive a heifer.

A stream of influence that found its way to the center of Europe developed during the Hungarian revolution. Brethren Service workers were in a conference close to the Hungarian border when they heard that refugees were fleeing across the border into Austria. The meeting adjourned, and soon Brethren Service was in operation along the border. The refugee camps around Linz that had been closed were re-opened. Brethren workers were invited to return to the camps. The old scenes of refugees making their way with meager belongings were repeated. Unlike those traveling after the war, these looked well fed. The Austrian government could not absorb all of those who came. Government agencies worked with others to free Austria of some responsibility by making arrangements to clear transportation as far as Canada and the United States. The immediate task for the service workers was to teach the English language and clear information and procedures.

Brethren Service followed the policy of using as many youth as possible, not only to give specific aid to persons in need but also to be present in as many communities as possible with a testimony of peace and goodwill. A representative of the young men and women serving in Greece said, "I worked primarily in the distribution of 900 bushels of hybrid corn to farmers in about forty villages. Since then I have been working with fifteen village men near the Albanian border on the cleaning of a drainage tunnel. The length of the tunnel was one thousand meters. During the week we stay in the village. We go to Ioannina on weekends to prepare for the next week and to report on the work of the previous week. There are eleven members on the team including a Dutch boy, a Swede, and a Greek girl."

At the very same time another volunteer was working at the Sandbostel (Germany) boys' refugee camp. He had the job of organizing and dispensing clothing that came through relief supplies. Also he had the task of fitting the clothing. He made regular visits to the new arrivals in camp, to help them get acquainted with the camp and its facilities and to invite them to vesper services and discussion groups. He wrote,

"I have met sharp and basic criticism of democracy here which has caused me to think and try to prepare myself better. The scale of work is vast, the obstacles are confusing and entangled and somewhat fatalistic in their pattern. One cannot avoid mixing with people at their level and viewpoint. I think it sobers one. An American who is quiet and interested, has a respectful but firm attitude, and does small things joyously, may not create an outward revolution, but he can touch the hearts of many."

Another young man, a builder, said: "My principal reason for joining with Brethren volunteer service was to come to Germany to finish the Kassel House, at Kassel, Germany. I first learned about the house when I spent Christmas with my sister there in 1951. It had been my ardent desire to help with the project, but unfortunately at that time I was working for my uncle then—Uncle Sam—or the United States Army. I decided that as soon as I was released I would come to Europe, provided they still needed builders.... On this job we worked from seven to five every work day. It was hard work, done in a completely different way. We had four German skilled masons working with us. These men were very patient with us Americans, for they had to put up with our mistakes, our English, and our outrageous German, besides teaching us the German way of doing things. Their greatest frustration was the way people came and went.... I have done a few exciting things in my short time here. Working on this house and associating with people here have undoubtedly been the best and highest experience of my life."

Another young man, at the same time, served in a hospital at Neuenkirchen (Germany). "Why do you do so much for me?" an old man asked him. "I am an old man who has lived his life and now wants to die. I have nothing and will never be well again, so why do you take care of me? You are an American, but you are here doing the unpleasantest of unpleasant work for the smallest amount of money."

Others were curious also. They knew the life they had lived. They heard about the life Americans are supposed to enjoy. But for an American to come without pay to do the work needed for mentally incurables and old people who were hopelessly ill was almost beyond their understanding. Then when the discussion led to the information that the youth is a conscientious objector, the question was, "Is this allowed in America?"

The witness of this young man is: "I am at the Evangelical hospital near Bremen, Germany, where I work in the infirmary of the institution which is made up of an old people's home, a children's home, hospital wards, and operating rooms. The patients that come to my ward are the ones with permanent injuries, sores, or sicknesses. This is the last stop in their life before being called home to their Master. In the eight months that I have been here I have never seen a patient being released as healed. Many times the way is not easy. There are trials and troubles.... Pleasant life? No, but one that can be made so if a person sees the work that must be done and can do it in the spirit of the Good Samaritan.

"As I live with these people of another country, I get to feeling as one of them and can get to be one of them, sharing alike in their sorrows and their tears. I have learned to know them as personal friends, people that I could never turn against. It is a two-sided friendship, each learning more about the other and binding the friendship so tight that it will help toward the brotherhood of man in the world of tomorrow."

A young woman worked as an office secretary at the Kassel house. She said: "I am in one of the jobs that is more or less behind the scenes. I am serving as a secretary to the director of the German program. Our offices are situated in the Kassel house where we also live and carry on all phases of our program. It is easy to forget the outside world. To help us remember the situation around us and also to help us learn the language better, every volunteer lives in the home of a German family for at least two months. All we need to do to really see the need is to work with the material aid department and help distribute food and clothing. We see destruction on all sides which daily reminds us of what we have to do."

A young man working in a family refugee camp at Loccum (Germany) expressed himself in these words: "I am located in a *Flüchtlingslager* outside a small village called Loccum, near Hannover. This German word means "refugee camp." But to me it means more. It means homeless people. Then it is also a blessing because the people have a roof over their heads and they are not starving physically because they have potatoes, bread, and *Wurst*. But they are starving for hope, for spiritual things. They come from all parts of the country. Some of the people had been very wealthy, and others very poor. My purpose is to try to raise the morale of these people by working and talking with them. . . . People stay here until there are jobs in sight, and because of so many well people in Germany without jobs it is sometimes hopeless for these old and handicapped people to find jobs. Therefore, many of them think they have nothing to look forward to, so they take the attitude, 'just don't care any longer.' "

Another young man served in Turkey near Istanbul. He wrote: "In Turkey, in cooperation with WCC a refugee program was set up to include the maintaining of a farm camp for a large percentage of refugees there. The farm is located on the Asiatic side of the straits of Bosphorus, about ten miles from Istanbul. The camp is located on the land of the summer palace of the last sultan. One hundred ten refugees live there. These refugees have escaped from their families and homes. The age range is between seven and seventy. Most are in good health and capable of working when there is opportunity. They cannot legally work in Turkey. The program of the camp demands the presence of two Brethren volunteers as a foreign team. The program which was intended to be farming turned out to be in the area of administration and recreation. The project, though psychologically difficult, is a challenge for Brethren volunteers as they rub shoulders with personalities from Bulgaria, Albania, and other countries in the strange and fascinating environment of modern Turkey."

"My work has all been within the city limits," a woman volunteer reported from Kassel. She was responsible for material aid distribution: "It has offered a variety of experiences. In cooperation with five welfare organizations — Red Cross, Catholic Welfare, Protestant Welfare, Labor Welfare, and the refugee office, [I have] the opportunity to prepare and distribute fifty food packages to fifty families each month. Each organization selects from the files the names of ten families that need help most urgently. They are invited to come to the distribution point where I have the chance to talk to the people and hear their stories. Each organization also sends the names of three or four families each month to whom we can personally deliver a package. There are always many new refugees coming from the east zone, and the living conditions are sometimes pathetically primitive. Clothing which comes from the United States is given through these five organizations. It is a thrill to be able to live with bales of clothing, bedding, for these welfare workers, and to work with them as they give to those who have so much need."

At the same time a young man in charge of the student exchange program wrote: "It has often been said that the teenage exchange program is to promote peace and understanding between the nations. We feel that the extent to which these people are able to fulfill this purpose is somewhat dependent upon the help we can give them before they go to the States. After their return to Germany and before they go to the States, the help which we can render consists of meeting and talking with them both in their homes and in conferences. We can answer questions which the students have regarding America, and particularly the Brethren in America. We are able to clarify and eliminate misunderstanding which has arisen from stories they have heard.

"The first three months in the States is a trying time. This is reflected in the letters the students write to their homes, their teachers, and their comrades in school. It is during visitation with the families at this time that we are able to explain these difficulties and help their parents to know the best way in which they can encourage the son or daughter. At the end of the student's year in America he has become accustomed to American life, habits, and customs. So much so, that he finds it hard to leave the American home to return to the native land. Students come back full of enthusiasm for the States, and sometimes attempt to convey their enthusiasm of what they have seen and heard in the States to their school comrades, to their parents, and to their neighbors. But the German people do not always accept it. There is some resistance to such enthusiasm. It is our task to meet with students in conferences, in work camps, by letter, and by visiting in the homes."

At this time one volunteer was working in a mobile service team of WCC in France and the flooded area of Holland. Others were involved in such activities as living in a youth village in a German city; doing social work in Kingsley Hall in London; acting as manager of a peace center at *Freundschaftsheim* in Bückeburg in Germany; helping on the reconstruction of a Protestant school in Vienna; distributing material aid in Vienna; doing the work of a nurse in a refugee health program in Upper Austria; working with material aid in Linz, Austria; performing refugee resettlement work both at Kassel and Linz; caring for German children in a nursery; teaching English and recreational work in Linz; and visiting where heifers had been distributed. In the meantime there were calls for nurses, secretaries, agricultural managers, social workers, builders, recreational leaders, hospital attendants, business managers, children's workers, youth leaders, and home economics teachers.

Qualifications? All should be undergirded in an unshakable faith in Jesus Christ and his way of love; all should be well in control of their emotions; all emotionally mature persons; all with a sense of humor (the world needs cheerful Christian service); all fortified with a robust service motive.

Another very important development was in work camps. The first one in Europe that the Church of the Brethren started was in the YMCA building in Heilbronn, Germany, for a local church. The theory was to bring people from different countries, not more than two Americans, sometimes a total of twenty or more, to work together on a specific project. Sometimes Catholic as well as Protestant churches were aided, and in needy places rehabilitation for refugees was furthered.

The reverse of having Brethren Service representatives in Europe involved the sending of hundreds of students to America, to live in homes in local communities. The BSC staff first became interested in the exchange program in Germany in 1948 when they placed three students in Brethren colleges in the United States for two years of study. In 1949 they took three more from Germany, making a total of six, in undergraduate schools. In January, 1949, following the report of an earlier program for twelve Polish agricultural students, the German program was discussed, which resulted in ninety German teenagers living for one year in American homes; in the following April and May nearly two hundred more were to go. They were located in fifteen states from the Atlantic to the Pacific. Brethren Service attempted to coordinate its activities in the local community with all organizations. These teenagers were selected on the basis of scholarship and personality traits. The whole program was worked out with the cultural exchange division of the American Forces at Bad Nauheim. Students came from Bavaria, Württemberg, Baden, Hesse, Bremen, Berlin, and a few from the British and French zones.

Dr. Alfred Lynch and Dr. Trude Gunther helped most in creating this program and initiating the plan. The food and agricultural division staff was also very cooperative, as was James Keim of the Stuttgart office, and Dr. Conrad Hammer who gave much time to this effort. Without the help of these officials it would have been difficult to have the plan approved and initiated. After the pattern was established—the sojourn in America proving satisfactory, and returning students reporting satisfaction to their parents and communities—the major difficulties were eliminated so that nearly a thousand youth found their way to America to participate in community life for one year and then return home to complete their education. Thus they gave their witness to one step toward peace.

Many other ways were found in various countries to build goodwill and friendship. But the teenager program seemed to offer the finest potential results because of the length of time the young people have to live to utilize the results of their experiences, both in foreign countries and in America. It will be nearly a half century before a true evaluation can be made of all that has gone into the effort to build an understanding between peoples who have been through the tensions of a world war.

4. A Visible Presence

by M. R. Zigler

Brethren Service personnel landed in Europe in 1945 with temporary headquarters in London, Paris, and then Brussels. With the coming of materials for distribution in Austria and Germany, accompanied by personnel, it was essential to establish facilities for operation by authorized persons. At first fraternization was forbidden with the German people. When the government changed its regulations so that there could be contacts directly between the government and the Austrian and German people, Brethren workers established their own quarters in order to eliminate the distress that resulted from living in houses needed by refugees and the homeless.

In Austria we found it difficult to locate places since renting or purchasing had to be authorized by the military government. In every country, for best operations we preferred to have administrative headquarters in the capital city, with easy access to authorized programs. For the most part, relief agencies had liaison persons who met regularly with government representatives. At the same time, the center of operations usually focused outside the capital city. Both General Lucius Clay for Berlin and General Mark Clark for Austria advised the Brethren to work outside the capital cities. Linz in Upper Austria was selected as one place to accommodate a staff of workers. Since Brethren Service was a new agency cooperating with administrators in government, the Austrian authorities approved a site on government property near the docks on the Danube where we could build a house for a temporary location. Built of materials procured from many sources since new lumber was not available, the house at Linz was a satisfactory place of residence although it was often very crowded.

The house at Kassel in Germany, like the house at Linz, represented the presence of Brethren Service on a national level and in some respects was a center for the operations of BSC in

Europe. We needed a place where staff members could come from the States and where the Brethren Service volunteers could get a firsthand vision of a destroyed city—to live in a house in the midst of destruction, with windowless and roofless buildings all about; to be in sight of a church spire without a sanctuary, of smokestacks without factories; to be within a stone's throw of mass cemeteries occasioned by a few minutes of mass bombing. Beyond the physical ruins, we became acquainted with people coming back to their homes that had been destroyed. Refugees by the thousands came from the East. In Kassel, within twenty miles of the east border, could be found every type of needy persons.

At the time of building the Kassel home (1952-53) the program was described as follows: "Over 1,000 families were assisted in immigration to America. Almost all of these have friends and relatives remaining in Europe. Over 700 heifers were given with no strings attached except those of Christian love. Thousands of pounds of food, clothing, and soap were given to needy people. Sun lamps, vitamins, shoe repair machinery, etc., were given to institutions. Over 500 youth have been reached through our international work camps. Close to 400 teenagers have been sponsored for a year's experience in America by Brethren Service, with 79 more to go in 1952-53. Indirectly thousands of German war prisoners were helped in camps. From the youth village at Kaltenstein which we helped get started, youth are graduating and acting as leaders in directing further youth villages. Several dozen youth have spent a year or two in Brethren colleges in America. A variety of contacts by Brethren Volunteer Service (BVS) workers have been made in hospitals, in refugee camps, in children's homes...."

The houses at Kassel and Linz were built by volunteers guided by engineers who could guarantee the work under building codes and regulations. The volunteers were young people for the most part untrained in carpentry and other aspects of construction. A builder from the United States came with his wife to Kassel to work under the direction of an architect from Göttingen. Two interpreters aided us; a woman, in working on the job; and a man, for purchasing materials and making contacts with city officials. Several locations were offered by city and church officials. A Protestant leader, Dekan

Schwab, proposed that the building be related to his office which was still in ruins. *Hilfswerk,* through Pastor Preuss, offered the possibility of relating to the offices of the Protestant social agency. Herr Geissen, a German citizen who had worked for Brethren Service for a number of years, also offered a location. We finally decided to build on ground that later would become a park.

The location within the park was over a bunker, and the land was covered with huge piles of rubble. Fortunately, the rubble could be leveled off and the excess pushed to the sloping side toward a lower street level, thus improving the entire park area. Anticipating the removal of all the rubble almost caused BSC to decline the offer to build in the park. But, fortunately, the military government let us know that it was necessary for the training of men in the military service to learn how to remove rubble. They said if Brethren Service would furnish the gasoline for the equipment and could find the GI's who would be willing to do the work, the necessary machinery could be utilized without cost. It is likely that this operation of moving rubble would have cost at least ten thousand dollars under a contract for the clearance. Furthermore, it would have been almost impossible to find equipment outside the military forces.

With the gradual increase of resources from the States and young men and women volunteers available to work under a supervisor, the large building at last became a reality. In two countries, therefore, Austria and Germany, the Church of the Brethren through BSC registered its presence. This created a stability for our program far beyond our fondest dreams. The Germans and Austrians stated that the fact that we built buildings indicated that we had come to stay. With a permanent address, Brethren Service became a reality. From these centers five programs were administered: BVS, work camps, exchangees, material aid, and the heifer project. They provided facilities to take care of files and records, to hold administrative conferences, to send personnel into fields of service, and to offer periods of relaxation and spiritual uplift when they would return.

After these buildings had been erected, Brethren Service had the qualities of stability and permanence. Neither of them was set up as an institution for local programs but as a place where the streams of life could mingle in fellowship, and through which the life and work of the church could flow. The local citizens and the "invaders" could work together. Though different ideologies were expressed, a unity of plan came into being through encounters in these houses.

The Linz house accommodated a dozen people beyond the staff. The Kassel center could house up to 125 students and had special rooms for guests. Both houses became known by city officials and the police, and individuals were often sent to the center for help. Above all else, there was one objective—peace and reconciliation, an objective that would last far beyond the giving of material aid, beyond rehabilitation and self-help, and on into the future until peace should be declared in the name of the Christian church. On the trail of peacemaking there was no turning back. Decisions regarding the implementation of goals and programs had to be judged by this longtime, life-giving purpose.

A third center was established at Geneva, Switzerland. It soon became clear that this should be the center of clearance for the total European operation. WCC had its headquarters here, and it was with this organization that the Brethren decided to integrate their program. Here were the headquarters of the international YMCA, the international YWCA, the World Student Christian Federation, and many worldwide agencies, including the United Nations offices for European affairs. The refugee program for the United Nations had its operations and headquarters in the old League of Nations building. Geneva was a favorable location from which to plan a world program and a European outreach.

The Brethren opened offices in Geneva and later moved to a permanent office in the WCC headquarters. The Presbyterian World Alliance and BSC utilized one of the temporary barracks provided by WCC. Here representatives of Brethren Service worked closely with the WCC staff members who thereby became aware of the development of our various programs of service.

Since Geneva was the place where the executive for the work in Europe should reside, we needed a meeting place for small gatherings, particularly in the interest of peace. We wanted facilities for overnight guests and strangers who came to Geneva from other countries, many times without sufficient funds to pay for normal accommodations in the city. Our head-quarters should offer a resting place and a place of opportunity for all church workers in Europe. By the time it became certain that Geneva would be the permanent place for the head-quarters of the World Council, we had already made our plans for administering our European work from Geneva.

The establishment of centers in Geneva, Linz, and Kassel not only registered our maturity in the minds of churches, governments, and the people in Europe with whom we had contact, but also in the total life of the Church of the Brethren in America. These centers were established in faith that contributions would be offered for the completion of the enter-prises.

The coming of BVS units guaranteed the human touch for the material aid program. The young people who volunteered time and energy in the construction of the centers of Kassel and Linz agreed with a statement offered in 1951 by Jerry Pence in speaking to the German staff there:

"We accept this challenge humbly when we survey the job of building and the biggest job of all, the one that is to be done when the building is completed, but we are sure that even un-der the pressures of world situations, this is perhaps the best way to work with our fellowmen in a neighborhood house to help alleviate some of the fears and doubts that come to us each day from the streets of Kassel. From now on this work will be considered of primary importance for the BVS unit. We view these tasks not as that of laying a brick or driving a nail, but that of creating with God's help a center where men may have a better understanding of his fellowman and of his God."

A minister sent a gift saying, "As my last act of the pastorate I am now leaving, we have collected a gift toward the Kassel house. This is a token of interest in Gundella, Marian-na, and Lore who lived for a year in our congregation, and the sincere interest we have in friendship and peace among all peo-ple everywhere." A statement of response to a similar gift read: "In expressing appreciation for a gift of $250, we are certain that we are building a $225,000 residence for $25,000. This week our American builder, sixty-year-old volunteer building master, with American fellows and German workers are put-ting in windows and helping on the plumbing, plastering, and electrical work inside the building. We have great dreams for the use of our house. We have 450 families in Germany who have a young person who has spent a year in an American home and has gone to high school and has participated in an American community. During the year there were 230 campers from twenty-two nations in seven different work camps. Right now we have many calls for American volunteers to serve in refugee camps, in hospitals, youth camps, and refugee homes for short periods of time. This center will be the base from which these people will go to all projects and where they will return in preparation for home-going."

A visitor from Geneva wrote: "Kassel gave me two different impressions. The first is something terrible, seeing the destruction of a town and all the great pains which are behind each stone and behind each window. The second is plenty of light. It is the work you are doing with all your collaborators, your sympathy with all the suffering people and comprehension of the human poverty. It is not always easy to follow the teaching of the Lord who demands that we practice the teaching to love our neighbor. This is the reason why I had such a luminous impression, seeing in what spirit you are doing your work."

In almost every operation the methods of the American builder and the American volunteers were different from those of the German people. An example of this is an experience the American builder had in regard to placing the rafters. The Germans felt that they should bring a large crew of workers on the next Monday, but the American builder, Roscoe Inman, had a great morale victory on Saturday, as reported by the director in Germany, Don Snider:

"On Friday evening the rafters were delivered. They were cut properly. But the German workmen just assumed that a special crew under Mr. Braun would be hired to come to assemble them. Mr. Inman politely informed them that if we had to wait until Monday they would not need to come because the rafters would be up. With the volunteer boys he worked all day Saturday and fit them together perfectly and in record time. When Mr. Braun came with his workers on Monday morning they could not believe what they saw. They rushed up to examine the work. 'I can understand how you might have done it, but I can't understand how you got these young kids to do it with you.' Equally surprised were the German workmen. Mr. Geissen kept saying on Saturday, 'You'd better invite Mr. Braun to come here and inspect; it won't cost anything.' Mr. Inman said, 'I think we can do it alone.'"

Almost constantly, German exchange students who had been in America for one year visited the Kassel center. One brought a friend with her when she stopped to have supper with the staff at Kassel house. They helped wash the dishes and spent the night. After breakfast and morning devotions, they said, "We are so thankful to you for the wonderful spirit of friendliness we find here. It is like having relatives in Kassel, to know that whenever we are here, we will find a welcome at Brethren house."

One US church furnished a gift for the building of the kitchen. The building foreman designed the kitchen personally. Two double sinks were donated by Brethren plumbers. A builder sent two Bendix dryers. A Maytag dealer who had been in Europe as a seagoing cowboy sent a new washing machine. A furniture manufacturer gave money for a good piano. A German Catholic layman who had an American exchange student in his home gave the linoleum for the floor at cost. The dedication date was October 23, 1953, the tenth anniversary of the huge air raid on Kassel that had killed twenty thousand civilians in one night.

Brethren young men serving with the US armed forces in Europe, occasionally visited Kassel house. Often they would bring with them German teenage youth whom they had learned to know in America. It was a great thing to help build friendship between the men in uniform and the German people.

So often serving in the relief and rehabilitation program caused some sadness, as in the early days when a building was evacuated for the residence of the Brethren Service staff and local people had to be transferred to lesser accommodations. When the initial steps were taken to locate the new Kassel center some very beautiful and rather large gardens had to be disturbed before harvest time. The records show that several prayers and short statements were made before digging into the beautiful gardens. An old lady who lost her potatoes stood by crying. Efforts were made to compensate the losses.

The Kassel building could not have been completed without the direction of one volunteer whose contribution was described, during the time of the building, in these words from the *Kasseler Zeitung:* "Also the work of Mr. Inman, the friendly building foreman from Ohio (United States) who has been called to Kassel for the sole purpose of building this house, requires only small costs; Mr. Inman, too, works as a volunteer and without pay mostly. He and his wife have been guests of the Brethren Service Commission for two months; he directs the building work and intends to stay at Kassel for two years in order to see the completion of the project. They hope to complete part of the house this year. Next year, new workers will come to their aid to complete the building of the home to which German youth will also have access. 'That they all may be one' is the inscription on the cornerstone which was dedicated recently."

The program now centered in the new facility at Kassel covered a number of areas. The executive in charge of the project at that time wrote to churches and individuals who had contributed, saying: "Today I drive 200 miles north to meet a cattle ship which brings heifers for relief in the interest of peace and goodwill. On the way I will visit a refugee camp in the east zone. Seven hundred came through last week. I will take four bales of shoes along for the political refugees coming from the west. Until this date 900 families had received heifers that were distributed over West Germany. On the way we visited a representative of the YMCA camp near Hannover where the German young men wanted to discuss conscientious objection to war. The week previous, four volunteers had visited the peace conference in Berlin and Holland...."

A newssheet called *Echoes* was established, and 450 copies of it were sent to the teenagers who had lived in Brethren homes in America for one year. By the time of the 250th anniversary of the Church of the Brethren in 1958, the staff of the Kassel center was in contact with thousands of people in Kassel and nearby. Intensive service was rendered not only in behalf of the Brethren but in cooperation with other agencies that had materials and resources. Beyond the Kassel vicinity there were more than a thousand exchangees who have been in the States for a year. Four thousand families had received one heifer each. Over three hundred volunteers from America had had experience in German homes and communities and on projects. Another long list of contacts were made through visitation and by letters. When all such contacts are recognized, it is apparent that the Brethren staff was in touch with 40,000 persons in the interest of relieving human suffering and in reconciliation, and in the ultimate purpose of establishing peace on earth in the name of Christ.

The purpose of the Kassel house—and of other centers that gave evidence of a visible Brethren presence in Europe—is well expressed in a letter from Don Snider to contributors to the building fund in September, 1952:

"Our Kassel house will be a place where we study the ways of peace as found in the New Testament. We will glorify the way of service to help build goodwill and better understanding between God's children. We fight against class divisions, against national prejudices, against racial discrimination, against church competition, against industrial evils that destroy man's spirit, against family disintegration. It will be our purpose to help men and women that hope to rise above their petty, selfish interests and be a part of the larger community which we believe can be identified as the kingdom of God. We constantly struggle to reach upward to these high levels of attitude and behavior ourselves, and follow the Master who has gone the same road."

5. A Personal Testimony

by M. R. Zigler

The Church of the Brethren, surviving more than two centuries, awakened after the Second World War to a sense of mission, based upon the message of the Good Samaritan and the vision of Matthew 25, upon the principle that these two New Testament directives had to be lifted from the traditional aspects of individual obedience to the teachings of Jesus to the obedience of a church as a body. Becoming a servant in the world of agonizing masses of people after the war, the church was searching for a promised land that had to be created, recognizing that it had to be both architect and builder for the future.

The records in this document reveal how this vision was implemented in a number of specific cases. They represent a small part of the potential achievement. In order that I may personally evaluate this specific effort of the church to be obedient as a servant, I must stand off, as it were, in distance. To do this I must return to my childhood days as I have observed the Church of the Brethren at work in the world and follow the light through to the present.

Through the centuries the Church of the Brethren endeavored to build a church made up of groups that were autonomous in their local communities. Often where two or three agreed to build a church, there a church was established. An individual who entered the fellowship promised to accept and follow the counsel of the group, which might be called a company of brethren. Disagreement with the counsel, ending in disobedience, had to conclude in disfellowship. It was understood by each member that the congregation did not expel a communicant, but the disobedient one himself chose to leave the group. By this method, according to tradition, the church kept itself pure and obedient to the common vision.

The church was opposed to certain worldly relationships. There was mutual care for one another, and physical and spiritual needs were provided by the group. In community affairs the members of the church did not ostracize themselves, but participated in schools and lived as citizens in the community in the accepted economic order. They took a definite stand against any form of violence in settling difficulties among themselves, and proclaimed this way of life as the message for the world in order to have peace. The mutual aid expressed in these groupings was not confined to the members of the group. Collectively they expressed their concern for others, joining in as helpfully as possible to meet the needs of the community.

The responsibility for teaching religion rested primarily in the home. Parents were held responsible for the teaching. Teaching was supplemented by preaching once a month, and a business meeting was held once a year to prepare the members of the church for a communion and love feast service. Without much literature beyond the Bible, without a paid ministry, this company of believers in the priesthood of all members formed a solid community of love that stood the test of the centuries.

These groups did not make a desperate effort to compete against other religious bodies. They sought religious liberty and granted it. They believed in closed communion, with trine immersion as the method of baptism; and the love feast with its three parts, first the feetwashing, second the meal, third the bread and the cup. Members of other congregations were invited and expected to join a local community, recognizing the fact that the church was made up of more than one local congregation although a local church was considered autonomous. In order that there might be an association of congregations an Annual Meeting came into being. The decisions of the group were then advisory to local congregations in their life and work.

In the rural community in which I was born, near a village of about five hundred people, there was a Mennonite group much like the Brethren but different in some respects. They believed in closed communion, as we did. In the village there were four churches—the Baptist, the Presbyterian, the Methodist, and the United Brethren. The Baptist Church practiced closed communion while the other churches opened their communion services to members of other churches. There was not much intermingling at the Lord's table in these churches, however. A thousand friends would sometimes come to observe a Brethren love feast, an annual event in the community.

In general, the church of my boyhood days seemed to have the spirit of religious liberty that granted freedom to others. There was not much concern as to how each practiced the teachings of the New Testament. There was a deep respect on the part of each denominational group for each other, as they tried to implement the aims and objectives of the various bodies in the community.

Because of some peculiar qualities of Mennonites and Brethren we were somewhat set aside from other groups, especially in reference to our position about nonparticipation in war. This was the one thing that occasioned the calling of the Church of the Brethren a sect rather than a church. Any young person belonging to the Church of the Brethren had to face criticism in school and community life. This naturally resulted in discussions of religion and community affairs.

It was not difficult to follow the Brethren trail through a college experience and a year in seminary and then into the First World War when the churches had to take a stand on war issues. A member of the Church of the Brethren did not go through this period without coming to grips in a realistic way regarding his commitment to nonviolence.

Before this time, while it was not clearly spoken, as a member of the church I felt that churches believing in war could conscientiously participate; that was their business. But members of the Church of the Brethren should not take part in war. Believing that I should do something during the period of the war, I was invited to become a YMCA secretary at Parris Island, South Carolina, with the United States Marines. There I observed the dedication of young men to the aims of war.

I had conversations with the leading commanders of the cantonment and revealed to them my convictions about war. One of the outstanding men said to me that he would like to have me visit him every Sunday evening when possible; a commanding officer was lonesome. One evening he said, "Don't preach to me, but pray for me." I replied, "If I cannot preach to you, what shall I pray about?" His reply was, "Pray that I shall never have to send my men into battle. But if I do have to order them to go, pray that they will fight vigorously and win." I found that he did not object to my position against war. I also discovered that few soldiers, if any, desire actual war. This officer said the churches could have prevented the First World War and wanted to know why they did not. "If there are going to be wars and rumors of wars," he said, "there are enough non-Christians in the world to perpetuate a conflict. A conflict should not occur among Christians."

From that moment in 1917 I believed he was right. When I was invited to become secretary of home missions in the Church of the Brethren, I accepted the call, although I was not prepared for it. I became interdenominationally minded and entered into the fellowship of interdenominational circles to proclaim the vision I had—that the churches of Christ could save the world from war, if they would be willing to eliminate violent methods in settling disputes, by each member of the churches individually taking the stand of nonparticipation.

When I arrived in Elgin, Illinois, in 1919 at the headquarters of the Church of the Brethren, at the age of twenty-seven, I had my first local contact with the larger churches—the Lutheran bodies and the Roman Catholics. The Church of the Brethren represented a very small body in Elgin and had no indigenous background as a base for developing the headquarters, which included a publishing house, general church headquarters offices, and a small local church membership.

After many years of rejecting higher education, foreign mission work, and the utilization of Sunday schools and Christian education, the church found itself equipped with a number of colleges and a seminary, indicating that the church was ready to move ahead in the world in practically every type of Christian enterprise known to the Protestant churches.

Experience through the centuries created the solid belief that the church was incarnating the gospel of Jesus Christ as a way of life revealed in the New Testament. The Church of the Brethren was gaining the trust of other church groups although our beliefs and practices varied from those of others. Always there was kept alive the idea that Christians should be a separate people from the world, but they should, as far as possible, go into all the world as creative citizens in governmental affairs and so live as to be trusted and creative in churchmanship.

These ideas seemed to come through the literature following World War I. The church found its way into the interdenominational circles of the Home Missions Council of

North America, the Foreign Missions Conference, and the International Council of Religious Education. This trend toward interdenominational fellowship was almost broken by the failure of the Interchurch World Movement in 1920. After some years, consideration was given to the church becoming a member of the Federal Council of Churches of Christ in America. This consumed many hours of discussion at two Annual Conferences before authorization was granted (1941).

Along with the resolution on the Federal Council of Churches there was attached a brief second consideration which read: "That when and if the World Council is organized we would seek membership." Therefore, when the World Council was organized, the issue involved was to appoint delegates to the World Assembly at Amsterdam (1948), which was done. Likely for the first time in history, the Church of the Brethren participated in the charter meeting of an interdenominational organization. This was not as easily attained as it appears. For a long time Brethren believed they should separate from the world and not be unequally yoked together with others. Other churches were often called the worldly churches.

Before Amsterdam the Church of the Brethren had sent delegates to the world assemblies in 1937—"Life and Work" at Oxford, England; "Faith and Order" at Edinburgh, Scotland. In these meetings at this high order of assemblies I discovered how many churches would not participate in communion except when in the traditions of their own church. I returned to Elgin to think again of what I saw there. It did not bother me that through the years the Church of the Brethren was not listed as a church but as a sect, and sometimes even under the word "others." Yet it was unbelievable how hard it was to get this nomenclature changed and to list the Church of the Brethren as other churches were listed.

All this came back to me when Bishop Lilje presented a report to the Central Committee of the WCC at St. Andrews, Scotland (1960). He raised the issue of what to do with the sects. The question came to my mind, What is a sect? I quickly remembered my first experience in Elgin with Lutherans and Catholics and their parochial schools, and with neighborhoods that were being careful that their children did not associate with others. Therefore I had to ask for the floor in the Central

Committee and inquire why it was that the Church of the Brethren was considered a sect when it cooperated in community affairs, could attend public schools, and did not attempt to take away the privilege of anyone to worship according to the dictates of his or her conscience. It occurred to me at that moment that the sectarians were those who had parochial schools and closed communion and other varieties of differences, all good and right and deserving protection. But I had come to the conclusion that all denominations were sectarian and should not be called churches. Or, putting it in a different way, all were churches and none was a sect.

If there is no recognized difference between church and sect, then the Church of the Brethren can sit in a chair at a conference table with other communions and place its testimony alongside the testimony of theirs as a part of the interpretation of the New Testament to meet the needs of our day. We have agreed to open communion, to invite other Christians to the Lord's table, and have opened the way to go to other Christian bodies when we are invited. In other aspects we have changed our ways and joined in the great movement toward a united declaration of the Christian faith in the world.

As I have observed the several denominations, I see that each is different from the others. These differences are considered sacred. Many are willing to die to maintain certain beliefs. This forms a kind of vision to be revealed, but at the same time becomes a stumbling block for a closer walk together along the highway of love. Probably the stumbling block that the Brethren hold dear and which gets us into difficulty, with churches and with governments, is our position on participation in war. This has been held since the beginning of the church in 1708. All Brethren hear the proclamation that we should not participate in war nor learn the art of war. We simply cannot understand why other Christians cannot declare this same doctrine.

Unless the Church of the Brethren loses its charter and breaks down its doctrine on peace, it cannot join other religious bodies in union until this question has due consideration and acceptance as the proclamation of all churches involved. In order that we may truly look forward to the time when we can hear the proclamation and blessing, "Blessed are the peacemakers, for they shall be called sons of God," the churches that believe in the sacredness of life cannot help but accept the tremendous obligation to make the world safe for a child to be born and to create a world in which to live so that the end of the life of every person can be marked as a total existence of joy and peace.

The Church of the Brethren, the Mennonites, Friends, and others, in several countries, have been able to secure religious freedom from governments for men who conscientiously believe they cannot participate in war. They have found ways and means whereby alternatives may be established that are satisfactory to the military and to the communities in which the young men live. Probably the most difficult agreements to be created between pacifists and nonpacifists are within the Christian order.

To the extent that every soldier committing himself must be willing to die for a cause, and to do inevitably something more difficult—kill someone whom he does not know—in the name of war, political proponents and theologians are demanding money and men at great sacrifice from all citizens. Such extravagant expenditure of life and resources in militarism has never been accepted by the proponents of peace who desire to live by the principles of Christ. The Church of the Brethren through the years has tried to implement Matthew 18: "If a brother sins against you, go and tell him his fault, between you and him alone. If he listens to you, you have gained your brother. But if he does not listen, take one or two others along with you, that every word may be confirmed by the evidence of two or three witnesses. If he refuses to listen to them, tell it to the church.... If two of you agree on earth about anything they ask, it will be done for them by my Father in heaven." This has been the way of keeping peace in the Church of the Brethren. We find that it is good when used in the right spirit, and we declare it as a means of settling the misunderstandings in the world.

Try to imagine what might occur if all churches agreed according to their own traditions to prepare for and carry through a universal communion service in each local congregation, with the end in view that we can at any time say that we have forgiven one another of all offenses and that we have approached every one for reconciliation where we know we have committed offenses. Preceding the communion service, a thoughtful and sincere examination service could be participated in at the sanctuaries, or in the homes, hospitals, or anywhere absent members could be located. In view of the fact that two great world wars have been fought in the center of Christendom by Christian men and women, it is clear that when this vast number of church members, including youth, would arise from the Lord's table there could not be continued grudges and hostility in the hearts of the participants. This would be a preparation for the promised assembly of the faithful in what is called eternal fellowship with God, as promised by Jesus Christ, the head of the church, whose body the churches represent on this earth.

The Church of the Brethren has found its greatest unity in serving together among the religious bodies since World War II in the interest of all suffering persons, without discrimination, and without a conscious attempt to proselyte for the Church of the Brethren. On the stateside, we joined in perhaps the highest fellowship with two organizations: (1) the Heifer Project, Inc., in which Catholics and Lutherans and other Protestant bodies associated with the Brethren until it became an interdenominational agency that could operate anywhere in the world; and (2) the Christian Rural Overseas Program, known as CROP, set up by an authorization of the American Council of Volunteer Agencies to be administered by the Mennonites and Brethren. Later the government said if the Catholics and Protestants worked together on such a project, the government would give authorization for the solicitation of farmers to send materials abroad. How they worked together is illustrated by an experience at a CRALOG meeting in Germany. A shipment of heifers was to arrive at Bremen to be sent to Austria. Transportation was provided to Bremen and from the German border to the destination in Austria. There was no money available for transportation across Germany. A few persons standing in the center of the room at coffee hour discussed ways and means to transfer the gift across Germany. In one corner of the room there was a Catholic representative, and in the opposite corner a Protestant. These two were invited to meet together in the center of the room and proposals were made that they might furnish the funds for the transfer. In a few moments this was agreed to and the cows were delivered in Austria and distributed to Catholic and Protestant farmers.

To Serve the Present Age

Is it not possible to call leaders from all religious faiths to assemble for discussion to unite on available resources and create an unbreakable commitment to eliminate war among men? We have learned to work together in distributing materials, in working out agreements with governments; we have been able to talk across all lines with religious bodies. We have found ourselves working in Berlin, in the villages of Germany and Austria, in Vienna, in Italy, in Greece, in Warsaw, in Beirut and Jerusalem, in Cairo and Rome, in Hong Kong and China, in Southeast Asia and Japan. In every nation of the earth the world is tired of war. There is awareness of the waste and expenditure of life and resources. The world waits for champions strong enough to lead out and bring reconciliation to the world. It is my belief that we have learned how to reconcile one another through service and that we are now at the point where all religious bodies are ready to say unitedly that we are reconciled to God, and that we love our neighbors as ourselves.

One of the thousands of families in need of food, clothing, and shelter in the years immediately following World War II.

Opposite, above: Church agencies help Spanish refugees who had fled to France in 1937-38. *Opposite, below left:* David Blickenstaff brings material aid to a children's home in Spain. *Opposite, below right:* Dan West was the first BSC worker in Spain. cooperating with AFSC. *Above:* The BSC in an early session: seated, left to right, H. F. Richards, M. R. Zigler, L. W. Shultz, Florence Fogelsanger Murphy; standing, Leland S. Brubaker, Paul H. Bowman, J. I. Baugher, Andrew W. Cordier, Paul W. Kinsel.

Above: Civilian public service camps brought together conscientious objectors assigned to "work of national importance." *Below:* Loading wood, a work activity at many CPS camps during World War II.

Above: Eager for overseas assignments, CPS men devote time to language study. *Below:* The first BSC project outside the continental U.S. was established at Castaner, Puerto Rico, in 1942.

Above: A group of German POW's arrive in West Germany following imprisonment in the USSR. *Opposite, above:* Returned German POW's are welcomed to a YMCA convalescent camp. *Opposite, below:* Luther Harshbarger, director of war-prisoner service in Germany confers with his successor, Werner Lott, himself a returned POW.

84

Opposite, above: Much material aid went to church-sponsored institutions. Refugees from East Germany at a home for the aged in Ludwigsburg eat a meal prepared from CROP flour. *Opposite, below:* Dr. Eldon R. Burke directs the work of CRALOG which combined the material aid activities of many agencies. *Above:* Food and clothing came from many countries; this stack contains materials from BSC, CWS, WCC, and other agencies. *Left:* Children learn that help comes through CROP from America.

86

Opposite, above: One of the registered Brown Swiss bulls sent to Greece by the Heifer Project in cooperation with the Near East Foundation to improve livestock blood lines. *Opposite, below:* M. R. Zigler meets children who will be aided by the gift of goats, purchased in Switzerland for distribution in Germany. *Above:* Benjamin B. Bushong, executive secretary of the Heifer Project Committee, watches as eleven heifers are loaded for Venezuela, the first HPI shipment to South America.

Above: A BVS training unit processes clothing for relief at the New Windsor Center (1955). *Left:* Trucks operating from New Windsor make regular visits to churches and other points to collect clothing.

Above: Donald E. Miller, material aid supervisor, delivers shoes to a youth in a refugee camp in Upper Austria (1953). *Below:* Cecile Burke manages preparation of garments from BSC-donated materials, Germany (1949).

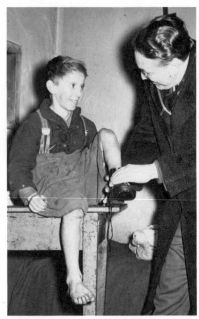

Left: W. Harold Row participates in clothing distribution while visiting BSC work in Ostroda, Poland (1947). *Below:* At the youth village in Kaltenstein Castle in Germany, endangered youth find ordered existence; Byron P. Royer assists them with clothing (1949).

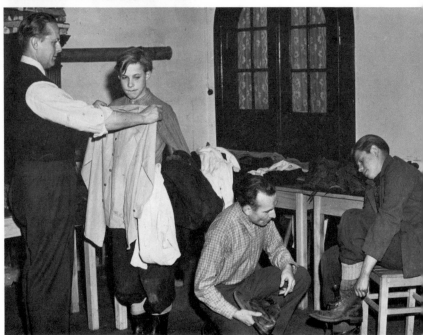

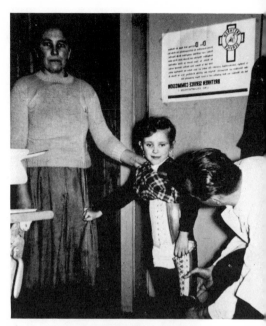

Right: A refugee girl is fitted with a prosthesis in the BSC clinic in Linz, Austria (1952). *Below:* Rosemary Block Rose, together with Dr. Zimmerman, visits patients in the Thalham TB Sanitorium, Austria.

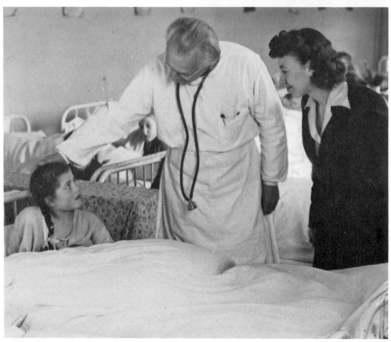

Above: The BSC project in Carrara, Italy, featured club activities for young people. Eula Lucore leads a knitting group. *Left:* Charles and Ruth Webb talk to neighboring children near their community center at Dunkerque, France (1948).

92

Above: Ellis Shenk, director of HELP project in Sardinia talks to a refugee resident (1966). *Below:* Inter-Church Service Team director Harley Kline distributes improved garden seed to village officials in Greece.

Opposite, above: Helena B. Kruger interviews a refugee family in Rome for the purposes of resettlement (1948). *Opposite, below:* Under the leadership of Ray Petersime, the Oakland Church of the Brethren in Ohio sponsored hundreds of DP families for resettlement in the U.S. Each year newcomers were honored in special gatherings, such as this Christmas party. *Above:* A unique resettlement project involved the Kalmuks, of Asiatic origin but of Soviet citizenship. BSC was asked by CWS to undertake the task.

Above: A BVS volunteer, Winoma Spurgeon (fourth from left) accompanies German and Austrian high-school-age students participating in the teen-age exchange project. *Opposite, above:* Carolyn Ikenberry spent a year in the home of a German family. *Opposite, below:* The first exchange program brought young Polish agricultural specialists to the U.S. for training and experience. The program continues, after a pause of some years.

Opposite, above: A Yugoslavian, a German, an Austrian pastor, and an American volunteer (Gale Crumrine) labor at construction at a work camp in Austria (1951). *Opposite, below:* One of the campers in a BSC-sponsored international work camp (1953) was Andrew Young, later the chief aide of Martin Luther King, Jr. and now a U.S. Congressman (second from right). *Above:* Work campers construct a new water system for the village of Schwarzenau in Germany (1954).

Above: Ethel Myer visits a neighborhood family during a summer work camp in the U.S. (1955). *Below:* Don Murray, who went on to a career in acting in Hollywood and on Broadway, helps build the Kassel BSC center while in BVS (1953).

PART TWO
STATEMENTS OF PARTICIPANTS

1. The Historic Peace Church Fellowship

by Orie O. Miller

Mennonites came through World War I knowing pretty well where we stood as a people of God on nonresistance, at least as our leaders interpreted the Scriptures then and until recently. Many of our forefathers came to this free America simply to avoid confronting Western Europe's growing militarism and the standard of interpretation was pretty well maintained but not with a very good witness. Most of our young men, when called up in line after the conscription act was passed in 1917, left more of an impression that "we won't" than an impression that "we cannot." So some of us in the period of 1918-25 were eager that if there should be a next time we would be better understood.

It seemed that the World War I conscription act was passed by Congress without much thought about the conscientious objector (CO). At least it is said that Secretary of War Newton Baker was quite surprised at the number of CO's and their firm stand. But he seemed flexible on that day and provided a way for the genuine religious objector to take that position and for his historic and his biblical reasons to be respected. The Friends seemingly were glad for the position and accepted alternate service for their sincere young folks, and the rebuilding of French villages destroyed by war was accepted by those in authority as legitimate service.

In the first seven years after World War I a number of efforts were made by Friends, Brethren, and Mennonites to think through the issues more clearly and to be ready to answer in keeping with the Christian position (as understood by us), so a number of joint meetings were held, mostly called by Friends and Brethren, but to which we also were invited and attended. We remember attending one in Washington, D. C., in 1922 to which practically all the Protestant denominations were invited and where Matthew 5:38-48 and Romans 12:21 were the heart of the discussion. There had been no experience with conscription since Civil War days, and many of our grandparents simply paid the taxes levied by law through which someone else was paid to go in the CO's stead.

About 1935, when many saw or at least felt the imminence of what turned out to be World War II, H. P. Krehbiel (Mennonite) arranged for representatives of the three peace church groups to meet with him in Newton, Kansas, for sharing of positions and for becoming able to say more clearly what was generally understood by us and why. About two hundred attended the meeting, and a strong statement of position resulted. This Newton meeting also provided for a Continuing Committee of three persons—one from each of the three peace churches—designated to think and work through the position to be taken, should there be conscription again.

After this committee met a few times, the value of small group meetings as such became clearer, and at each meeting general plans were made for the next time and for inviting special interest folks from the three churches to meet with us; usually a total of about twenty met each time. We have in our archives minute records of these and of who met—one time they might have been representatives of our church colleges, another time overseas missionaries at home on furlough, and at another perhaps representatives of our publication interests.

The first Brethren representatives were L. W. Shultz and C. Ray Keim. The Friends sent Errol T. Elliott, from the Five Years Meeting of Friends in the middle west territory, and Robert W. Balderston. From about 1941 on, M. R. Zigler became the Brethren representative on this committee. He had the reputation of bringing peace into every talk he gave, whatever the subject or place. Clarence E. Pickett, executive secretary of AFSC at that time, through his personal acquaintanceship with President and Mrs. Franklin D. Roosevelt, helped much in making clearer the scriptural position taken.

About the same time Paul Comly French, who was well acquainted with government decision-making, was very helpful to us all in Washington, D. C., in the development of the CPS idea and its acceptable development. Zigler, with his deep convictions on the position, helped much with the weakness and gaps in legislation proposed and in developing guidelines for our later implementation of the World War II conscription act of 1940. It was earlier agreed that the religious objector respect the privilege of the act, which continued through World War II and was administered for the government by the Selective Service system.

The Friends decided that their main objection was to conscription itself, and so as the NSBRO was set up, they took their share of the financial costs and met with the board regularly, but usually as observers only, while Brethren and Mennonites shared equally in the total costs of the board's work all through World War II. The National Service Board also provided for representation of the Fellowship of Reconciliation (FOR) and for representation on the board itself by any other group in the United States feeling inclined to be so represented. So there were annual meetings of the board itself while the active representation, or executive committee work, was done by the smaller groups who had taken on the day-to-day responsibilities as worked out between the board and Selective Service for the CPS camps. Each of the three church groups operated camps and served anyone who wanted to join these.

The objections to the camp system were: (1) no provision was made then for overseas service except what was worked through by Andrew Cordier in Puerto Rico, and (2) after some experience with the several types of conscientious objectors the whole concept was altered somewhat and provision made for broader services, such as mental hospitals and other social services calling for special training. (There were a number in the forestry and conservation camps who had more specialized training.) Later postwar versions of the conscription act allowed for a wider acceptance of conscientious objection and a wider range of services, including overseas services. There were many later who took positions of criticism toward governmental definitions of conscientious objection comparable to that of some objectors during the Vietnam war. The structure of the service board in Washington also reflects this. The Roman Catholic position on war, which provided for what is known as the "just war" position, was also taken note of. As experience accumulated, the range of alternative service allowable was much enlarged by the government.

Also, during World War II war bond purchases, a plan by which society in general could make more money available for war, lay more and more heavily upon many hearts and consciences. A little was done at that time on the war bond question, but so far, nothing has been done cooperatively regarding war taxes. The tendency of the peace church agencies, however, was to respect the tender conscience, which still seems right and consistent.

Besides sharing equally in the overhead expenses of NSBRO (now the National Interreligious Service Board for Conscientious Objectors), Brethren and Mennonites did a number of other things cooperatively. One example is the CPS program in Puerto Rico. One could also mention particular projects in Southern Ohio, and of course some cooperative programs developed later in Austria and Greece in all of which the Brethren carried the larger financial load but seemingly always gladly. As Mennonites, we always appreciated this opportunity to work closely with the Brethren projects; M. R. Zigler's quick, clear thinking on the issues involved gave joy to us personally; we remember life's close friendship with M. R. Zigler and others. And one sincerely hopes and prays that as time goes on these two Christian groups will add their strengths, minimize their differences, and symbolize in many ways the feelings between us which surfaced through World War II.

2. Cooperation With the AFSC in Spain

by Dan West (d. 1971)

Civil **war** has been destroying the country that was
Spain. Two years ago twenty-four million persons lived
there, but more than a million have been killed. More than a
million soldiers—perhaps 600,000 on each side—are now
attempting to destroy each other. There are said to be three
million refugees, and more than a million of them are children.

This bitter struggle grew out of a deep-seated conflict
between classes; it is part of an old story, too. This is the third
civil war in slightly over a century. Whatever the merits of
either party, now it is an endurance test with suffering increasing on both sides. Several times there has been talk of
some kind of an armistice, but it has not happened yet.
Meanwhile the killing goes on and hunger takes a growing toll
of the lives of innocents.

Early in 1936 several English Quakers were concerned
about beginning goodwill work in Madrid, but after the war
broke out that could not happen. And so efforts were made to
help care for the children in and around Barcelona. Several influential Spaniards also became interested in the possibility of
help and in a short time there grew the English Quaker Service.
From England in October, 1936, came word for help from
America. After some thinking and planning together by
representatives of the Friends, Brethren, Mennonites, and the
Federal Council of Churches, Sylvester Jones was sent to see
about the need and the chances for nonpartisan work on both
sides of the conflict. When his report was approved one worker
was sent to each side in May, 1937. Others have been sent since
as the work has developed.

Editor's Note: Although this article differs in type from others in this
book, as a contemporary account rather than a memoir, it does provide a
good picture of the work of the peace churches in Spain and is therefore included. It appeared originally in the December 19, 1938 issue of *The Gospel
Messenger.*

Cooperation With the AFSC in Spain

At present there are twelve workers from America in Spain in the cooperative project, nine on the Loyalist (government) side and three on the Insurgent (Franco) side. Three of them are Dunkers. Miss Martha Rupel works at the hospital in Murcia (Loyalist Spain). She has been there since early August. David Blickenstaff has his headquarters at Bilbao; he has been there since early December, 1937. Paul Bowman [Jr.] sailed from New York on October 28, to work with him on the Franco side.

Over here is a Committee on Spain with headquarters at 20 South 12th Street, Philadelphia, Pennsylvania. It is composed of several Friends, Mrs. R. D. Murphy, M. R. Zigler, and Dan West from our church, Orie Miller of the Mennonite Central Committee, and Roswell Barnes of the Federal Council. John Reich, the secretary, carries the main burden of the work. The Friends Service Council of London has workers in Barcelona, Murcia, and elsewhere. We consider ourselves a unit with them, as our peace testimony is one, and so are our essential purposes. The Spaniards call us all "Quaqueros," and they are grateful for the help we are giving their children.

Many outside agencies are helping there, and both governments have extensive plans to save the suffering civilians. But it is wartime, and all that every agency can do will not keep them all alive. How many must die this winter [1938] no one knows—but thousands certainly, likely tens of thousands. Since they cannot all be saved we have developed the policy: "Save the children first"—the neediest children in the neediest places in the neediest regions. This means refugee children on each side first, who are far from home and most helpless. Dependent mothers and old people are cared for, too, but not first. On the Loyalist side the need is far greater; and so we are doing more there. Because of the different conditions we are maintaining some hospitals, colonies, workshops, and schools, but they are not first; and we are not expanding these. We must save the children first, and that means feeding them first. As winter comes on we will give out clothing—to the neediest children first.

On the Franco side we worked most in the mountains of the north last winter. (It was colder weather than Chicago had.) In the spring we worked along the Ebro near Belchite, Lerida, and Teruel—the neediest places. On the Loyalist side we are working in and around Barcelona and Murcia. The former territory is filled with refugees from northern Spain who came over through France more than a year ago. The English workers are still doing most of it there. Our work is done mostly in the region around Murcia where refugees have come there from central and southern Spain. Perhaps that is the neediest region of the whole country, as most of the other agencies from outside Spain are not working there.

In a letter from Murcia, September 27 [1938] Florence Conard writes:

"Some time ago I was at the hospital for supper with the English nurses. After the meal, they slipped into the babies' room to see a little tyke that they didn't think would last the night. The child was supposed to be suffering from kidney trouble, but was actually an excellent example of a typical 'war baby.' It was about six months old, its head one third of all its tiny body. Its arms, I'm not exaggerating, were no bigger around than my forefinger and its loosely-covered fingers just hung from the wrists. Its eyes and cheeks were sunken and its jaw and cheek bones were so prominent as to seem completely naked of skin. Already it had begun to gasp a bit for breath, moving its head back and forth on the pillow as though the very motion would give it more air. Calcium was lacking in its body among other things. No bomb holes, or refugees, or women's tears and sob stories can move me so much as that struggling little life, so helpless against external diabolical forces. Just a P. S., the baby died."

Never before have I known what food really meant. Not roast pork and mashed potatoes, not good American ice cream, not even spinach and lettuce and cabbage—just food, with no particular taste or form—fuel and nourishment for the weakening flesh.

Bread! Only now am I beginning to understand the meaning of "Give us this day our daily bread." (Perhaps our "daily bread" today is but 100 grams—3½ ounces, but father and mother will pool their grams, forget their hunger and give the extra pieces to the young ones. Tomorrow, God willing, "our daily bread" may be 150 grams. We cannot bear to think that perhaps tomorrow there will be no bread. It may be wiser not to think of the morrow. "Give us this day our daily bread."

Not long ago ten, long-looked-for tons of wheat arrived.

Cooperation With the AFSC in Spain

The men staggered in under the weight of the big sacks and dumped them in limp piles in our warehouse. The little puffs of dust that squirted out from between the sacks as they fell, seemed to hang still and golden on the air. Yesterday the bread from the wheat came in—good bread, brown bread, wheat bread, symbol of health and strength and work, of plenty and friendship and peace.

3. The Formation of the Brethren Service Committee

by L. W. Shultz

Brethren Service has its origin in the words of our Lord: "I was hungry and you gave me food, I was thirsty and you gave me drink, I was a stranger and you welcomed me, I was naked and you clothed me, I was sick and you visited me, I was in prison and you came to me" (Matt. 25:35-36).

As a boy I can remember the response the Brethren gave to calls for aid in Armenian relief, India famine, and China relief needs. The church gave generously. During the first World War the Brethren were active in counseling those in army camps or prisons. An active Central Service Committee was formed having W. J. Swigart, J. M. Henry, I. W. Taylor, and C. D. Bonsack as members. An active Peace Committee also reported for years following 1918. About 1925 this committee seems to have been discontinued.

In 1932 the Annual Conference was held at Anderson, Indiana. At this conference the Brethren youth, then known as the Brethren Young People's Department (BYPD), held a meeting known as the Young People's Congress. At the meeting of the Youth Congress a petition to the entire conference was framed. As a member of the Board of Religious Education (later known as the Board of Christian Education) I was able to get this petition before the Annual Conference. The adoption of this petition really then became the basis for the very large expansion of the peace and relief work of the church for the next ten years and on through the ensuing third of a century:

"We, the Young People's Congress of the BYPD assembled at Anderson, Indiana, petition the 1932 Annual Conference through the Board of Religious Education as follows:

"1. To build up a church program of international goodwill.

"2. To investigate and provide a program of service in

cooperation with the Friends or others in establishing special arrangements for neutral relief work in time of war or periods of national crises.

"3. To authorize the Board of Religious Education to make the necessary investigation and build up the program needed for the above action."

The above request by the BYPD was carefully considered by the Board of Religious Education, approved and passed to the Conference through Standing Committee. The answer at Annual Conference was "Request granted."

The Board of Christian Education assigned to the Manchester College faculty the emphasis on peace. C. Ray Keim, L. W. Shultz, and O. W. Neher were appointed to promote peace education and the producing of peace literature for the church. Also, they were to work with the Friends and Mennonites in planning strategy for the crises that were appearing on the world horizon. Already in 1935 an important meeting of the historic peace churches was held at Newton, Kansas. I remember saying to Ray Keim that the time certainly was here for another meeting of the historic peace churches, and that it would appear that the Mennonites of Kansas should be the hosts this time. Accordingly, he wrote to the Krehbiel brothers who were publishers at Newton, asking them if they would send out the invitation, which they did. There was a good response, and in this meeting C. Ernest Davis and Rufus D. Bowman led out. A Continuation Committee was appointed which later became the NSBRO. This continues even today, for many denominations have joined it.

In 1936 the Peace Committee (Keim, Shultz, and Neher) with the Friends and Mennonites presented a message to the Quadrennial Methodist Conference at Columbus, Ohio. This message was very well received and may have had a good response in the later Methodist efforts in promoting peace.

At the 1939 fall meeting of the General Board of Christian Education at Elgin, Illinois, a proposal was made by some young leaders in the church to form a service committee on the same basis as AFSC with no corporate connection with the Church of the Brethren. We knew that this would never be agreeable to the church. M. R. Zigler asked me to go to my hotel room that night and frame a plan by which the committee would be a part of the church organization and receive the backing of the church. I did that, and on the next day the plan passed both the Board of Christian Education and the General Mission Board. Then it was approved by the Joint Boards, and in 1940 the Annual Conference approved the receiving of requests and reports directly from the committee.

The plan proposed in 1939 was that the two Boards—the General Mission Board and the Board of Christian Education—should comprise the church Committee on Peace and Relief and that they should choose an executive committee from the two boards to be known as the Brethren Service Committee. This served from November, 1939, to August, 1941. In 1941 the La Verne Annual Conference made the committee a regular board of the church organization. The membership at that time was: L. W. Shultz (chairman), Paul W. Kinsel, Andrew W. Cordier, W. Newton Long, Frank S. Carper, M. R. Zigler, J. A. Robinson, and J. I. Baugher.

As war clouds gathered and plans for conscription began in 1939, the Continuation Committee of the historic peace churches asked Joe Weaver of the Mennonites and L. W. Shultz of the Brethren to seek out prospective places in Ohio and Indiana for CPS camps to care for conscientious objectors. In late 1940 Weaver and I went to the US Army headquarters in Chillicothe, Ohio, and Indianapolis, Indiana, and there conferred with the colonels in charge. From these conferences it was recommended that camps might be planned in the Civilian Conservation Corps (CCC) camps at Marietta and Yellow Springs, Ohio, and at Bluffton, Lagro, and Medaryville, Indiana. These sites were accepted and by May, 1941, camps were in session.

Before the campers came in 1941 we had a staff ready to go at Lagro—with J. Clyde Forney in charge. They were there several weeks with no campers. At a Washington meeting with Gen. Lewis B. Hershey and representatives of the peace churches, I asked in a public meeting, "General Hershey, when may we expect draftees to arrive in our camp at Lagro?" He did not give me an answer. In about fifteen minutes I arose again and asked the same question. This time he responded. His answer was, "You know we are new at this job of handling conscientious objectors. We have not had the over two hundred years of experience that you peace folks have had. Please be patient with us for we do not yet know when the procedures will bring your first campers to Lagro." That question and his answer proved valuable in later events in the CPS camp experience.

Brethren Service has literally taken Brethren to all parts of the world. By the hundreds and thousands men and women have responded to calls to give, go, and serve in areas of great need.

Here are a few outstanding personal memories:

I well remember the adoption of the myrtlewood service cup at the Asheville, North Carolina, Annual Conference in 1942, as well as the service symbol and the service certificates. At Camp Mack in the years following hundreds of dollars were raised through the cups on the dining room tables. The hands in the symbol on the cup were those of Charles D. Bonsack and J. E. Miller.

I remember while at Muncie, Indiana, a call from W. Harold Row came asking me to serve as foreman on a cattle boat to Poland in 1945. At Baltimore, Deputy Premier Stanislaw Mikolajczyk of Poland came to the boat to see the cattle and said he would have a car ready to take some of us to Warsaw; I made a visit to his office in the capital of Poland. A year later I made the same trip with M. R. Zigler. I remember the two long car rides by night from Danzig (December, 1945) to Warsaw with no lights along the road in the countryside— seeing only ruins of houses, tanks, and planes.

I recall the two nights at Warsaw in 1945 in the home of Stanislaw Wegierick where there was no heat or food, where we slept in all our clothes. We foraged two mornings for breakfast on bread and Polish sausage (leaving some for the family, more than we had eaten for the two breakfasts).

My 1946 interpreter and guide was Stanislaw Bilinski (now in Washington, D. C.) who for eight days guided us in Poland, asking us "Why are you here? Why did the farmers of America give these heifers? Do you know this sounds like Christianity?"

I remember taking a $1,000 check in 1946 from the people of Warsaw, Indiana, to be given to the people of Warsaw, Poland, through their Mayor Stanislaw Tolwinski.

There were two little girls on the dock at Kiel, Germany, in 1945 as we looked down from the ship—the *Santiago Iglesias*—who looked to be the same size and were dressed alike. I said to them, "Sind Sie Zwillinge?" Their answer was

"Ja." That meant they were twins. Then, "Wie heissen Sie?" (What is your name?), and the answer "Schulz." Their name was Shultz also. What a thrill! We gave them a can of meat. What a Christmas treat for them!

I recall the day in 1944 when BSC met at New Windsor and purchased the Blue Ridge College property for a service center, little dreaming of its great potential.

There was the forenoon spent in December, 1946, in Warsaw, Poland, arranging for seven permits and visas to get me to Brussels to a meeting of the European workers, arriving at the last consulate as the door was being locked but kept open long enough for me to get a visa, then getting to the train for Paris just in time, only to wait two hours for it to start. I reached Brussels thirty-six hours late one night but found the workers still waiting up for me. Then I accompanied Bruce and Clara Wood to Warsaw and Ostroda, Poland. At Christmastime I spoke on a Sunday three times through an interpreter in a church with no heat, wearing everything but a hat, in a community building, and in an orphanage school.

I met Capt. Alexander Mack of the Moore-McCormack line in January, 1947, in Gdynia when I tried to find return passage for three of my 1946 party who had stayed with me for six weeks after the UNRRA ship returned. He was an officer who gave graciously of his help then and again in 1949 on our first tour.

I remember the day in the Schwarzenau *Bahnhof* lunchroom when the Brethren Tour No. 1 (1949) started a fund for a memorial in Schwarzenau for the remembrance of the beginning of the Church of the Brethren there. The idea was carried to Annual Conference and was accepted. The *Alexander Mack Schule* was built and dedicated in 1956 and was well noted in the 250th Anniversary held there in 1958.

4. The Inception of NSBRO and CPS during World War II

by Grant M. Stoltzfus (d. 1974)

While a summer student at Elizabethtown College in June, 1940, I was one of a small group who huddled around the dormitory radio to listen far into the night to reports that told of the fall of France. It came as no surprise to learn that on July 10 a bill was introduced into the House of Representatives "to protect the integrity and institutions of the United States through a system of selective compulsory military training and service." I had come of age in the late 1930s and noted the rise of dictatorships in Europe and Japan. I had read *All Quiet on the Western Front*. And I had listened to men tell of the brutalities they endured in military camps of World War I because they were non-cooperating conscientious objectors. By the late 1930s many Americans became convinced that war with Germany and Japan was "on the wave of the future." Reluctantly, I suppose I also had become convinced.

It was in this context that I learned from Orie O. Miller of the creation of NSBRO in the autumn of 1940. This board, I was told, included not only the historic peace groups but also Protestant leaders who spoke for those conscientious objectors who were largely the outgrowth of the peace movement of the twenties and thirties. In retrospect it becomes clear that this broadening of the base of conscientious objection was to be one of the important achievements of the NSBRO.

How was the broad base laid for the NSBRO? The answer lies in the two types of peace movements that grew up between the wars—movements in which Brethren leaders played an important role. The first began with the occasional meetings of peace church leaders in the twenties and thirties on the campuses of Church of the Brethren colleges, such as Manchester, Juniata, Blue Ridge, and Elizabethtown. Leaders and speakers at these conferences came from the CO ranks of World War I—mostly Quaker, Brethren, and Mennonite. In 1935 peace spokesmen from these three groups met at Bethel College,

North Newton, Kansas, in a more urgent mood than at previous meetings of the preceding decade and a half. The occasion was none other than the rise of Hitler in Germany and the threat of war that loomed over a rearming Europe. At this landmark meeting apparently the term "historic peace churches" was coined; an ongoing organization or continuing committee was formed by the three bodies; and in all the deliberations the possibility of World War II was grimly acknowledged.

Events which led to the formation of NSBRO moved rapidly after 1935. In 1937 Paul H. Bowman and Rufus D. Bowman were the Brethren members of a seven-man delegation of historic peace church leaders who interviewed President Franklin D. Roosevelt concerning peace convictions. The appointment was arranged for on the initiative of Clarence Pickett, executive secretary of AFSC. In January, 1940, only a few months after World War II began in Europe, both the Bowmans joined in a second delegation to call on President Roosevelt and this time left with the chief executive a memorandum that, among other things, proposed forms of nonmilitary service that might be substituted for conscientious objectors:

Relief of war sufferers.

Relief of refugees of evacuated civilian population.

Reconstruction of war-stricken areas.

Resettlement of refugees.

Reclamation or forestry services in the United States or elsewhere.

Relief or reconstruction work in local communities in the United States.

Medical and health services in connection with any of these projects.

Farm service.

Many efforts reflected Church of the Brethren peace concerns: a role in the 1935 conference at North Newton, Kansas; the creation of a Committee on Legal Counsel for Conscientious Objectors in the same year; the peace caravans in the 1930s as part of a vigorous peace education program; and the participation in the interviews with President Roosevelt.

There was a second movement which was to merge with the historic peace groups, and in this combination the Church of the Brethren, and M. R. Zigler in particular, played a part. The strength of this movement was the Protestant peace concern that flourished between the Treaty of Versailles and Hitler's invasion of Poland. One aspect of this movement was an anxiety about the status conscientious objectors from the nonhistoric peace groups would have in the event of conscription. Such a concern was all but unknown in World War I among Protestants.

It is therefore remarkable that in November, 1939, over two years before Pearl Harbor, a delegation of Protestant churchmen interviewed Attorney General Frank Murphy. Among these were Bishop G. Bromley Oxnam of the Methodists and Dr. Walter W. Van Kirk of the Federal Council of Churches. Their main burden was that conscientious objectors in the case of conscription or war be responsible to civil and not to military agencies of the government.

Dr. Van Kirk on March 11, 1940, wrote to M. R. Zigler to tell him that the Executive Committee of the Federal Council of Churches was of a mind to "convene a conference for the purpose of blueprinting a course of action for the conscientious objector." Van Kirk posed a question to Zigler: "Do you agree with me in this and have you any suggestions regarding the personnel of the Committee in the event the Executive Committee authorizes me to act? I am assuming that you will be the representative of the Church of the Brethren. Whom would you suggest might represent the other pacifist churches?"

M. R. Zigler replied on April 1, 1940, affirmatively to Van Kirk's proposal saying that: "The conscientious objector group has been delaying too long to think through and measure the spiritual power it possesses." In the same month Zigler asked Clarence Pickett to speak at the Brethren Annual Conference, saying, "Of course we would like for you to recognize the teamwork that is being developed among the Historic Peace Churches."

On April 19 Zigler conveyed to O. O. Miller of the MCC an invitation to meet unofficially with the newly-formed BSC. Further consolidation of the peace churches was implied in a July 3, 1940, communication to O. O. Miller and Harold S. Bender to join with Friends and Brethren to explore needs in Europe as the war began to spread its devastation.

Thus during the fateful year of 1940 a groundwork was

laid for a structure that was to be inclusive of both the historic peace churches and an emerging Protestant peace movement which "produced" conscientious objectors between World War I and II. Later events were to see wide differences in the spectrum of religious bodies as to aims and purposes, as to attitudes toward government, as to where conscience draws the line. But in the creation of NSBRO an instrument was forged that stood the strain of the war years by providing alternative service, the chief purpose of the Board's founding in October, 1940.

The idea of such a body interacting with the government and CO groups was a bold, new venture and no one was quite sure how it would work. Much vision and talent for the undertaking were supplied by the Society of Friends and its experienced, well-known agency, AFSC. In Paul Comly French, a Quaker and a seasoned newspaperman as well as former state director of a writer's project for the Works Progress Administration, the NSBRO had a capable and resourceful executive secretary.

Conscientious objection was recognized, to be sure, but would it be tolerated? Could it measure up to what it asked for itself? On November 8, 1940 (over half a year before the first CPS camp was opened at Patapsco, Maryland) M. R. Zigler wrote to D. W. Kurtz, "The nearer I get to this problem the more nervous I become as to how we can make good under our own supervision."

When I first heard of NSBRO in the autumn of 1940 I shared the enthusiasm of many that at long last there was service possible for the CO apart from the military. There was even a prospect of relief and reconstruction work to be supervised by the peace churches with the pacifist segment of Protestantism cooperating.

I was soon to learn something, however, of the problems of the peacemaker in wartime. In July, 1941, I met M. R. Zigler for the first time at a district meeting of the Church of the Brethren in Palmyra, Pennsylvania. He had addressed the meeting on the challenge of CPS for the Brethren and in conversation afterwards he commented on some of the "nuts and bolts" problems of establishing camps for "work of national importance." But he was hopeful for the program as a channel for pacifist convictions.

The Inception of NSBRO and CPS during World War II

The next memory I have of NSBRO was in March, 1942, only three months after the United States entry into the war. The occasion was a meeting of the board in the Florida Avenue Friends Meetinghouse in Washington, D. C. The problem that had arisen came from what Zigler as early as July 11, 1941 called "heavy pressure from the Methodists, Presbyterians, and others that the Government shall finance these camps for us." The seriousness of the problem for the historic peace groups, who were the numerical and financial backbone of the National Service Board, lay in the fear expressed by Zigler in his July 11, 1941, communication to BSC: "The question is: Can the Government finance without supervision and would we rather finance it ourselves in order to supervise our own camps?"

In the course of the meeting Bishop G. Bromley Oxnam spoke for the Federal Council of Churches in the vein that since the Government conscripted the men it should bear the costs of administering the program; and he felt the point was important enough to press before the Congress. Responses to Bishop Oxnam came from Paul J. Furnas of AFSC and Arthur Swift of FOR, both members of NSBRO. In brief but clear presentations they defended the role of the peace churches in administering a program independent of government finances. Then followed a tense session with the future of alternative service in the balance. All through the give-and-take discussions M. R. Zigler presided skillfully with all parties concerned given a chance to ask questions and probe into how conscientious objectors were to "be handled."

The day closed open-ended. Would the church-administered program of alternative service survive? Or would General Lewis B. Hershey, director of the Selective Service System, favor an appeal to the Congress for funds to operate CO camps? There was some fear (mostly on the part of the peace church men) that to reopen the CO issue in Congress now that the nation was at war was to risk losing the hard-won gains of both exemption and alternative service. The war was in its early stage for the United States. Toward the end of the last session Zigler commented that in this war, unlike World War I, American Legion posts dotted the map and such bodies could turn out to be quite unfriendly toward conscientious objectors. Public opinion would go either way, for or against the dissenter from war. As the war deepened we should expect somber horizons.

How the alternative service program fared as the war unfolded is a story told elsewhere, and much of it is yet to be told. Though the role of NSBRO was debated and some of its cherished goals were thwarted (foreign reconstruction units in particular), in and through the give-and-take with Selective Service a constructive and viable program of service in conservation, agricultural service, and significant mental hospital experiments went on. Opinions differ as to how well the historic peace churches kept their integrity in such close collaboration with the government—being, as it were, a cog in the conscription gears of a nation at war. The severe critics of cooperation, who favored prison over CPS, regretfully were not always regarded by other participants as co-workers in the same cause; nor did these absolutist critics always see that conscience seems to dictate differently to different people.

The NSBRO in this country corresponded to the Central Board for Conscientious Objectors in England, also of World War II vintage. The CBCO was more an organization *for* CO's than an organization *of* CO's, to quote its chairman, Fenner Brockway. Like NSBRO its strength lay in religious organizations such as the Society of Friends, the FOR, and many CO's of World War I. Both the British and American organizations came about because of the lessons of futility learned in World War I's unfortunate handling of the CO. Both performed legislative, administrative, and informative services for the CO's of their nation during years when mobilization for total war saw their respective states assume the most totalitarian form.

The NSBRO in the turbulent years of World War II had not only to keep unity of purpose amid the diversity of persons who sat around its council table. It also had to pioneer for broader and more effective forms of service for about 12,000 young men of all temperaments, faiths, and frustrations. It had to relate to government personnel, who, though technically civilian in status, were often military in outlook. The NSBRO had to move into an uncharted sea as it sought for a kind of "moral equivalent" amidst the acute tensions of war. It all added up to a big order. But church-operated alternative service persisted throughout the war, and invaluable lessons were learned that extended into the postwar period when the peace churches could come into their own in worldwide relief and reconstruction.

The important contribution of BSC and its chief spokesman, M. R. Zigler, to the NSBRO would seem to be that they furnished leadership and a channel for Brethren peace convictions. But the committee and M. R. Zigler also had a kind of catalytic influence as they collaborated with both the more separatistic Mennonites on the one hand and the Society of Friends and Protestant pacifists on the other. Through it all the various groups of NSBRO retained a high degree of their own identity; together they formed a united front, the first of its kind in the modern phase of Christian pacifism.

5. Japanese-American Resettlement Work

by Mary Blocher Smeltzer

Pearl **Harbor Day**—Sunday, December 7, 1941—is a day many of us remember in detail, including exactly where we were and what we were doing. At the time, Ralph and I were teaching school and living in East Los Angeles. For us, it marked the beginning of our interest and activity in the plight of Japanese Americans on the West Coast during World War II. Very soon public and military pressure began to mount "to do something about the 'Japs' on the Coast," who could easily be identified by their slant-eyes (even though this included a few Chinese). Rumors of espionage and sabotage were generated, but none was ever proved to be true. To this day, however, some West Coast residents believe that Japanese Americans were living purposefully at strategic intersections or military positions in California according to some master plan of the Japanese government. Demands for evacuation grew, encouraged by the Hearst press, Caucasian vegetable and nursery growers, and Lt. General John B. Dewitt, West Coast military commander. National security then became the pretext for the evacuation of the 110,000 Japanese Americans living on the West Coast.

During the winter of 1941-42 we attended monthly meetings of the AFSC in Southern California. Many Friends were concerned about the Japanese problem. We hoped also to involve the Brethren in the concern. M. R. ("Bob") Zigler attended the February regional conference in La Verne. As we were taking him back to Los Angeles, he asked us to keep him informed as to the developments regarding Japanese Americans. We sent him frequent reports, and I can remember more than once driving downtown to the Los Angeles post office in the middle of the night to mail Bob a report.

The first Japanese Americans to be evacuated were those living on Terminal Island, a fishing colony located in San Pedro—the Los Angeles harbor. They were given a forty-eight-hour notice in February, 1942, to dispose of their possessions and move out. Ralph took a day off from school to help. He had already been demoted from a regular to a substitute teacher in the Los Angeles schools because he expressed his conscientious objection to selling defense stamps. He was shocked at seeing army jeeps with machine guns patrolling the streets while looters were raiding houses from the alleys. The Quakers rented an abandoned school near our home to use as a temporary hostel for many Terminal Island refugees and their belongings. Within a few weeks all Japanese Americans in the Los Angeles area were evacuated, usually early in the mornings. We helped serve them breakfast at the train and bus stations, getting up at five o'clock, helping at the stations, then hurrying off to school.

First stop for evacuees was an "assembly center" such as Santa Anita Race Track, Arcadia, or the Los Angeles County Fair Grounds in Pomona. Horse stalls and hastily-built barracks were used to house them. Some stalls had not been properly cleaned. But after they were cleaned and used for a while, they proved to be better quarters than some of the barracks with large cracks through which the wind blew.

Whereas the evacuees were taken from the metropolitan areas in the spring of 1942, those in rural areas were moved in the summer. While we were directing a summer work camp in Farmersville near Lindsay in the San Joaquin Valley, Japanese Americans were taken from that inland area now classified as Zone 2. Some Japanese-American farmers from the Coast had relocated there earlier expecting to be safe from evacuation. We organized efforts to provide food and transportation to the train station in order to make the leaving a little easier for the evacuees. Although the military leaders welcomed our help, veterans, legionnaires, and local police harassed us and even threatened our lives. The situation was so serious that all helpers were called together early on evacuation day to reconsider our plans and have a prayer meeting. We decided that Christianity was on trial in Lindsay that day, and we must go ahead. Our tormentors surrounded us at the train station, shook their fists, and hurled derogatory remarks, but did not harm us.

Gradually all West-Coast Japanese Americans were put into ten War Relocation Centers in out-of-the-way places east of the Sierras, in California, Arizona, Utah, Colorado, Idaho, Wyoming, and Arkansas. We decided to apply to teach school at the Manzanar Center northeast of Mt. Whitney near Lone Pine, California. We were given civil service appointments, one to teach high school mathematics, and the other science. School opened in October in Block Number Two, consisting of about ten barracks each divided into four to six school rooms. We started teaching in empty rooms. Students brought newspapers to sit on the floor as they leaned against the walls. We had one set of books for all our classes. In spite of all the handicaps this proved to be one of the easiest teaching situations we ever had. Students were well-motivated and self-disciplined.

Life in Manzanar, however, was very oppressive to most "detainees" as well as to the Caucasian administrators and teachers. Caucasian personnel were housed in two separate blocks at the corner of the center and were not encouraged to fraternize with evacuees. Some staff had apartments with cooking facilities, but most ate in the Caucasian mess hall where meals were provided by the government at nominal cost.

About 10,000 Japanese Americans lived in the one square mile center, surrounded by barbed wire, guard towers, sentries, and searchlights. It consisted of thirty-six blocks, each with fourteen barracks, with each barrack divided into four to six apartments. Each block had its own mess hall; in the center of each block were two bathhouses, a laundry room, and an ironing room. Most bathhouses had a *nihonburo* (Japanese bath)—a large tub four feet by six feet, and two to three feet deep. The *nihonburo* was usually full of warm water. A number of persons would get in and soak at once. Some people spent many evening hours there.

The first Sunday that we attended church in Manzanar we met Mrs. Yato, the woman from whom we purchased fruit and vegetables in our local neighborhood store in Los Angeles. It was a great surprise and source of satisfaction to meet an unexpected friend there even under "center circumstances." We participated regularly in the Protestant church program and helped provide leadership for the Youth Forum and Young Adults. At first there was no *Nisei* (second generation) minister, and the services were not meeting the needs of the younger residents. There were also Catholic and Buddhist churches. Some services were in Japanese, some in English.

We came to feel very uncomfortable living in separated and better conditions than the Japanese Americans. We pressed the administration to let us live outside the Caucasian compound. Finally we were made "house parents" for a group of twenty *Kibei* fellows (persons born in the US, educated in Japan, and less Americanized than most Japanese Americans). Their dorm was sponsored by the Manzanar Center YMCA but called the YMA.

We had a large room at one end of a barrack. The boys occupied the rest with a hall down the center and small rooms on each side. We were in Block 36, Barrack 14, Apt. 1—the farthest possible block and barrack from the other *Hakujim,* as the Caucasians were called. We had good times and good relationships with the young men, enjoying their music and art. One gave us a priceless set of twelve water color paintings of Manzanar scenes. We ate with them in Block 36 mess hall every Saturday night, but took the rest of our meals with the *Hakujin.*

Perhaps the most unforgettable experience in Manzanar was the riot in December, 1942. The Japanese-American Citizens' League (JACL) had just held a conference in Denver, which some of the residents of Manzanar with American citizenship attended. This intensified the continuing conflict between pro-American and pro-Japanese factions in the camp. A mass rally protesting government treatment of Japanese Americans was held on a Sunday afternoon near the gate and administration buildings of the center. The soldiers on guard tried to disperse the crowd with tear gas. As the residents were leaving some trigger-happy soldiers shot into the crowd. Two Japanese Americans were killed, one a high school boy shot in the back.

That evening the camp became very tense. The anti-American faction vowed to kill pro-American leaders. A friend two doors from us came over frantically asking Ralph to find her husband who was hiding at his brother's apartment and to take him to the guard house for safety. Ralph took our Model A Ford, found him, had him crouch down on the car floor, drove without lights around the edge of the camp, and made a beeline across a field to the outside-gate guard house. Although they arrived safely, the guards said that if they had been on their toes they would have shot at the car. About sixty were rescued from the camp during the night and housed in the military compound. The army and AFSC arranged housing for them in Death Valley.

During the time we lived in Manzanar, it became clear to many other people inside and outside the camps that the Japanese Americans did not need to be incarcerated behind barbed wire, but should be relocated to jobs and freedom in the east. At first the only way a person could get out of camp was to secure a job before leaving. For most this was practically impossible to do. In January we helped Thomas Temple, a Manzanar staff member, make arrangements to take a group of young men from Manzanar to Chicago and to stay at Bethany Biblical Seminary. He was so successful in finding jobs for them that we and the Quakers finally received permission from the War Relocation Authority (WRA) to open relocation hostels in Chicago. Ralph and I made arrangements through BSC, chaired by Andrew Cordier and directed by Bob Zigler, to set up a Brethren hostel at Bethany Seminary.

In March, 1942, I took two fellows and a girl by bus and train to Chicago to start the hostel. I started out with three fellows but one skipped out on us and stayed with a friend in Reno, Nevada. He later appeared at the hostel. When he moved out of the hostel he gave us the largest box of chocolate-covered nuts and candies we have ever seen.

The students and faculty at Bethany gave us a hearty welcome. All of us ate with the single students in the boarding club. Later one of our hostelers, Shiz Akinaga, became boarding club cook. On April 2, Ralph arrived with four more hostelers. They drove to Chicago visiting four other relocation centers en route. We already had a sizable group at Bethany and were operating full steam.

The WRA opened a relocation office in Chicago to assist resettlers in finding jobs. Procedures were set up for persons in the relocation centers to apply to a hostel of their choice. In time hostels were set up in other cities: in Cleveland by the Baptists, in Minneapolis by the Lutherans, in Cincinnati and elsewhere.

Bethany gave us two rooms on the first floor of the administration building for a hostel office. We employed Virginia Asaka (Morimitsu), whom we had known in Manzanar, as hostel secretary. She handled most of the applications from the camps. Ralph and I counseled hostelers about jobs and housing. Single persons had a much easier time than families. It took quite a brave person to come to a strange city after having been locked up for six to eighteen months. Many families in the centers felt it risky to let their children in their twenties go out alone into a hostile unknown world. The hostel served as a bridge, a safe and secure place to begin a new life from the standpoint of both those coming out and their families remaining in camp.

Coffee and Eny Oshima arrived in Chicago with a family of several small children. The family was the subject of a photographic display made by the Brethren to advertise the hostel, to acquaint others with the project, and to help raise money for it. They returned to Sacramento after the war to pursue their business. The Oshimas lived in a Bethany apartment during the summer.

The Sim Togasaki family lived in the apartment behind the Brethren Fellowship House a few blocks away and became a part of the First Church of the Brethren, Chicago. Sim now has an import-export business in San Francisco, lives in Berkeley, and is an active member of the Oakland Church of the Brethren. Sim has served on the Church of the Brethren General Board.

Mr. Minowa was known as the man with the "smiling eyes"—they were blue. He was half German, half Japanese. I have never known a more kindly, more gentle, older man. He became ill at the hostel and it was necessary for me to take him to Cook County General Hospital. I will never forget the look on the faces of the hospital staff when I asked to admit him. It was as if there could never have been a worse combination then to be both a "Jap" and a German.

The hostel continued at Bethany until the fall of 1942. The student body, down because of the war, was now increasing, so we had to look for new quarters. We located an old mansion at 6118 North Sheridan Road, close to the lake, which had been a rest home. We leased it and agreed to purchase the furniture which was in good condition. Included were about twenty single beds—metal cots. All hostel residents moved to Sheridan Road. Bertha and Charles Kimmel joined us to help with meals, housekeeping, repairs, and the like. The Kimmels were adult volunteers who had been employed in CPS administration.

By April, 1944, we had helped more than 1,000 Japanese Americans come to the Chicago area. We were idealistic and working hard to integrate everyone into an ongoing community. We felt that we and others had helped enough Japanese Americans come to the area. We did not want to help create another "Little Tokyo" as there had been in Los Angeles and other West Coast cities. After consulting with an interdenominational committee and the WRA we decided to close our Chicago hostel and open a new one in Brooklyn, New York, even though we had renewed the lease on our Sheridan Road house. We were able to cancel the lease with a penalty, and BSC moved the furniture to the Fellowship House just opening in Elgin (another one of Bob Zigler's projects). The Kimmels moved there to get things started.

J. Henry Carpenter, executive of the Brooklyn Council of Churches, helped us find a fraternity house near downtown Brooklyn. Soon after we leased it, we ran into public relations problems. The house was located in an area of doctors' and dentists' offices. Because of fear and prejudice none of them wanted us nearby. New York's Mayor LaGuardia and New Jersey's Governor Edge also publicly opposed any such resettlement project, even though we had received the encouragement and cooperation of the WRA. Local newspapers carried frequent articles for a month regarding the hostel and related problems. The New York WRA administrator finally called us into his office to review the situation, pointing out the threats that had been made to our lives and property. He offered to allow us to back out of the resettlement project, but we declined.

Members of the press camped on our doorstep the day the first hostelers arrived and their picture made page one of the *Brooklyn Eagle*. A policeman posted himself at our door both for our protection and for surveillance. For weeks we had regular police visits recording all our hostelers and where they moved to. After a period of time the policeman began walking around the block. Gradually we were generally accepted and could operate in normal fashion.

In May, Bob Zigler visited the Brooklyn Hostel. He surprised us by coming up with the idea that he needed Ralph to be his assistant in Elgin. It seems as if Bob must have had pretty good control of us because it did not take us long to decide to move to Elgin. Perhaps the fact that we were expecting our first child in about three months helped us to decide. Cecile Burke took over as director of the hostel and carried on the program for about two more years.

As I reflect on our work with the Japanese Americans, I have a stronger feeling than ever that the entire evacuation was a very evil and unjustified affair. No matter what we, M. R. Zigler, or the Church of the Brethren did, this deep scar will remain on our history—an event that says much about us as a nation.

6. Work With Prisoners of War

by Luther H. Harshbarger

The invitation to write a memoir of my involvement with BSC and the World's YMCA's services to prisoners of war sent me scurrying to fragments of diaries and correspondence which stir up memories of persons, places, events, experiences of pathos, tragedy, irony, and joy which I try to forget 364 days of the year. I have learned from experience over the intervening years that a passing thought or an occasional event opens a flood tide of recollections of bombs and torpedos, spies, cages, rags, and mutilations, and the world that returns is a far cry from the bucolic scene outside the window of my farmhouse on a Sunday afternoon.

Sometimes it is difficult to remember, in view of the violence of the intervening decades, that the cessation of hostilities in 1945 left the European continent seething with a vast populace of the exiled and enslaved, wandering to and fro, waiting for transport to return to homes that in thousands of cases ceased to exist. Men were without machines, machines without fuel. Great areas of land lay waste, while whole peoples were wracked with famine and pestilence. Suppressed hostilities broke out in flaming fire and violence. In the heart of this seething cauldron was Germany in whose destruction men of many nations had found common purpose; in whose ruins they could rejoice, even if it meant their own ruin. Germany, in effect, became a vacuum into which other peoples poured their hatred and venom until it threatened to engulf them.

But Germany was not alone. The whole world was to see the rise of a "barracks civilization" and migrant cultures as more or less permanent features of international existence. To the twentieth century belongs the dubious distinction of killing more people and creating more refugees than all the other nineteen centuries of the Common Era. The year 1945 is, therefore, a symbolic date to mark the cultural shift from an epoch of habitation, in Martin Buber's terms, to an epoch of homelessness.

This statement may seem a rather vast backdrop for personal reflection, but these grim realities are the context for our story, and apart from such historical perspective, the story itself does not make a great deal of sense. Of course, prisoners of war are only one category of citizens of barracks civilizations, and in terms of military logistics, POW camps represent a form of solid waste disposal for the duration. It is obvious that an onrushing army in the wake of bombed destruction leaves a wasteland dotted by barbed wire enclosures. But one should hastily add that British and American treatment of prisoners of war in World War II and thereafter was the most humane in the history of warfare.

The Geneva Convention in 1929 had set the terms for prisoner of war treatment. Under these terms, in 1939 the International Red Cross Committee and the World's YMCA were assigned exclusive responsibility for services to and care for prisoners of war. The International Red Cross was responsible for legal rights, health, and physical condition of prisoners of war, while the World's YMCA was assigned the responsibility for their "spiritual and cultural welfare." For a decade, therefore, beginning in 1939, the World's YMCA as representative of all national YMCA's in the world, through its War Prisoners Aid (WPA), worked in sixty-three countries, a program that was to expand into services to refugees, displaced persons, *Wanderjugend* (wandering young) and other roving populations, political prisoners such as people classified as war criminals and civilian internees—in fact all those who inhabited this barracks civilization—the tragic victims of the epoch of homelessness. But our story must focus on POW's.

The WPA, valiantly and naively as it appears now in historical perspective, set as its goal to serve "till the last man is free." Its neutral position and relatively exclusive authority enabled it to be a catalytic agent which rallied to its cause people, money, material aid from all parts of the world; their nationals, war funds, churches and religious groups representing the ecumenical spectrum including Quakers, Mennonites, and Brethren. It is against that background at that "torpid turn of the world," in the decade of the 1940s, that the story of

Brethren service to POW's can be told. Some day the story should be written in its entirety for it is a part of the drama of our history which should not be forgotten.

However, our story here is and must of necessity be, a personal one. My first recollection of work with POW's goes back to the Ocean Grove Annual Conference in 1940 which my wife and I attended at the end of our first year at Yale Divinity School. By chance we sat in on a group where John Barwick was speaking on the eve of his departure for Great Britain. My memory of what was said is dim at best, although I still have a vivid memory of John Barwick's serious intent. But beyond that I had no idea what was involved nor that his mission had anything whatsoever to do with the World's YMCA. Therefore, it came as something of a surprise four years later when, as a BSC appointee, I was assigned to be the assistant director of the WPA in Great Britain where Barwick had been working during the war.

The BSC connection with the World's YMCA is due to three men: Tracy Strong, M. R. Zigler, and John W. Barwick. Tracy Strong, the general secretary of the World's Alliance of YMCA's, was an international diplomat who had a particular genius for selecting people, thrusting them into situations beyond their depth, and surprising to them for the most part, realizing his expectations. He was also the first to understand the multiplying effect and extension of services made possible by deploying persons from other organizations.

M. R. Zigler, as we all know, had a passion for feeding the hungry, clothing the naked, and now, in this connection, extending his passion, if not to proclaiming liberty to the captives, at least to visiting them in prison. John W. Barwick was a fascinating combination of the mystical and political and a genius who had the creative imagination and the skill to open doors and initiate programs for "enemy" POW's, which was to shape our work in Western Europe. The story of Brethren Service to POW's is the lengthened shadow of these men and the people they have appointed, trained, supervised, and supported.

A program developed as by an inner logic of its own, a logic which meets each situation on its own terms. All cages are similar, and the POW mentality is pretty much the same the world over. And yet, the years and the places brought vast differences related to the actual situation and the historical moment. In practice, "spiritual and cultural welfare" came to mean anything from ping-pong balls to Bibles to liturgical equipment. In reflection I can distinguish three periods of programmatic development: during the war, the postwar period, and the repatriation period.

When I arrived in Great Britain in January, 1945, there were approximately 350,000 Germans and thousands of Italian prisoners, some of whom had been in prison since Mussolini's ill-fated foray into Ethiopia in the 1930's. On the Continent, of course, there had been thousands, hundreds of thousands of American, British, and other Allied prisoners held in occupied territories or in Germany. The WPA was serving on both sides. Our services consisted of supplying all sorts of recreational equipment and facilities including sports, artistic equipment, musical instruments, libraries, but above all, and more significant, were the secretaries who worked on a regular schedule of camp visitations on both sides.

All of our work was done with limited resources available during wartime and under the constraints of military security. Every secretary or camp visitor had to accept as a condition of his mission these realities. We can all agree that the caging of human beings in barbed wire enclosures is an unmitigated evil. Yet we were not to ask why they were there, or when they would be freed. Our task was to serve them while they were there. This kind of constraint calls for a high degree of discipline, and not all people could meet the test. The temptation was either to become calloused or sentimental.

Naturally enough during the wartime period, secretaries for camp visitation were largely chosen from neutral nationalities such as the Swiss and Swedes, although there were other nationalities as well. On the whole, the British and Americans did the administrative and programmatic tasks outside the camps while these people were assigned to camp visitation. As the end of hostilities neared, however, I remember visiting several camps with persons like Pastor Julius Rieger, who at the time was pastor of the German church in London and who had been a Berlin pastor and a refugee. I recall that during my early visits with him as he conducted services in the camps, I wondered about all that I had heard about the atheism of Nazis and the Germans in general as I heard them sing "von Ewigkeit zu Ewigkeit" with tears streaming down their faces.

I remember also visiting camps in Scotland with Pastor Heinz Golzen. One was a *Luftwaffe* camp at Comrie the day after VE (Victory in Europe) Day, and I was shocked to discover that the pride of Hitler's air force simply did not believe that the war could have been lost. I also remember attending a funeral in the Edinburgh Castle on VE Day. A German POW had died of tuberculosis one day before the end of hostilities. Another of our camp secretaries with whom I was often associated was Sam Ybargoyen, a Uruguayan resident in France, the father-in-law of David Blickenstaff. Ybargoyen almost literally gave his life for the service, having traveled for three years in the dead of Scottish winters and, after receiving a visa to return to France late in the war, died on the doorstep of his home.

Basically the task during this period was one of amelioration of the prisoners' lot in all the ways under our command; they especially welcomed a neutral and civilian face from outside the enclosure. It was a time of waiting, waiting for escape, for the end of the war, for going home. It was also a time of great educational opportunities for those who could meet the test. Under the aegis of WPA thousands of Italian prisoners, for example, received the equivalent of a high school diploma through the Cambridge examinations. Many, many Germans passed their *Abitur* (high school graduation examinations) and men on both sides of the conflict literally acquired college educations. In the salvage operations after the collapse of the Third Reich, for example, it was not uncommon to recover from camps libraries of 20,000 volumes.

Early in my career in Britain, under Barwick's imaginative leadership, we developed the notion of a program oriented toward the rehabilitation and reconstruction of Germany. That meant that we resolved to follow the men in successive stages back to Germany, and to prepare them for contributing to the reconstruction of their own nation. We had formed the Joint Committee on Education for Prisoner of War Camps consisting of distinguished educators from among the German refugees in Britain who, along with British educators, advised us on the developing of an educational program. We set up a printing press at Luton which published thousands of textbooks, fiction, theological books, etc., a surplus of which was later sold under our aegis in Germany.

We made a value judgment that a ruined Germany would need most of all three types of persons: those who would go into education, youth work, and the churches. We, therefore, set out to establish a teachers' training institute, a youth training center, and a theological seminary for both Catholic and Protestant students. This brought about what may well be unique in the history of warfare: the establishment of the YMCA POW Camp under the sponsorship of the British War Office. Security was provided by the British Army, but the internal life of the camp was under the complete control of the WPA staff and the prisoners themselves. Here these three institutions quickly got under way, and eventually graduates of these institutes found their way into appropriate positions in war-torn Germany.

The war over, the character of the task changed. Paradoxically, with the decline of fighting, and especially after VE Day, the number of POW enclosures in Western Europe actually increased, thus expanding greatly the burden of WPA which had to meet this expansion with declining resources. The rapidity of the Allied advance, once the back of the German army had been broken, left Western Europe dotted with hundreds of crude, quickly constructed enclosures for thousands of POW's. Sometimes camps were held together by single strands of barbed wire, men guarded by their own officers, often with no more than a pint of water per day for all their drinking and sanitary needs. Shortly after VE Day I was dispatched to Belgium, Holland, and Germany on an inspection tour, and was absolutely appalled at the physical condition of these men, many times standing knee deep in mud. As I recall, there were 400,000 to 500,000 POW's in Belgium and Holland alone, another 700,000 in Western Germany, in addition to about 600,000 displaced persons (DP's) and refugees who had flocked into the Low Countries in the hope of some kind of relocation.

It was in the midst of this inspection tour that I was called back to Brussels to be informed by Hugo Cedergren, associate general secretary of the World's YMCA, that I had been appointed senior representative of the World's YMCA in Belgium and Holland. My mandate included not only services to POW's, but also the establishment of programs for refugees,

DP's, political internees and the like, as well as collaboration with the British YMCA, then operating out of Brussels, and the Belgian and Dutch YMCA's. It would take us too far afield to go into the details of the initiation of this program. It will be enough for our purpose to highlight a number of items.

1. In the summer of 1945 Dwight Horner became the associate director of WPA and Eldon Burke combined the task of educational director with setting up a relief program for BSC. Helena Kruger was assigned the task of working at the repatriation centers for refugees in a suburb of Brussels. For a period of about six months our headquarters in Brussels acted also as the relief headquarters both for BSC and MCC.

2. Within the year we established an office in Amsterdam under the direction of Dr. Frans Kooijman, the general secretary of the Dutch YMCA, charged with primary attention to refugees and camps for Dutch collaborators, and especially for their children who, we were informed by one Dutch officer, were born Nazis! Alice Burke joined the staff there for a time. Margaret L. Watson (later Mrs. Kooijman), a Scotswoman who had been on the WPA staff in England and Belgium, and Lois Rupel worked with several outstanding Dutch members of the staff for a period of approximately two years.

3. Of major concern here were the types of POW's whom we finally came to serve. We discovered in a survey that there were approximately 5,000 boys under the age of sixteen who had been gathered up in the last roundup, so to speak, and brought to POW camps in Belgium. As a matter of fact, we discovered also that our youngest prisoner was ten years of age and the oldest eighty-three. We were able to place these 5,000 boys on a large Belgian estate and, after selection of German teachers, established in effect a boys' academy for approximately six months before they were repatriated. The second type of prisoner who stood out were the general-staff officers who were captured in Germany and placed at Zedelghem near Bruges. My first visit to that camp was memorable. I walked into a barracks room to find approximately fifteen generals hovering over a large map of Europe and sticking pins into various locations. When I inquired what they were doing, they announced that they were planning a strategy for the World War III invasion of Russia! That was the level of reality at this particular point in the month of June, 1945.

My visits, however, were to have fateful consequences because eventually I established a discussion group with a half dozen of these officers, one of whom was to play an important role in our whole repatriation program in Germany. There was the captain of Hitler's private yacht. There was Admiral F. Ruge who had been an aide to General Rommel on the Western front, who was later assigned to the US Historical Commission and wrote four important books on the history of military affairs in Germany. There was Colonel-General Joachim von Arnim from the prestigious Junker family, and, last but not least, was Lieutenant-General Wilhelm Philipps, the chief of ordnance of the *Wehrmacht,* who was later to become the manager of our warehouses in Germany.

By midsummer of 1946 we were receiving a third and new class of POW's. These were men from Allied camps in America, Canada, Egypt, and other parts of the world who thought they were in process of repatriation, only to discover that they had been assigned to Belgium as reparations laborers. This may be a new thing in the history of modern warfare. It was not exactly slave labor, but under the terms of the Yalta agreement labor was included as one of the items of reparation: so 75,000 German POW's were assigned to Belgium to work in the mines. It takes little imagination to understand the moral and spiritual condition of men so caught in the tension of terror and emancipation.

We quickly set up our usual program of services, but in addition, developed a fairly sophisticated program of publications including two journals, *Tieflot* (10,000 per month) and *Querschnitt* (35,000 per month), and small books which were intended for the home library of the POW when he returned. These were written and edited by Germans under the editorship of Kurt Doering, who was to become an influential writer in Germany. I wrote a biweekly piece. Philippe Vernier, the well-known French pacifist, author of *With the Master* which he wrote during twenty-five months of solitary confinement as a CO, then a pastor in Charleroi, contributed regularly.

Morale was low, however, not only because the prisoners were detained at labor at very small wages, as dictated by the Geneva Convention, but also because of the dreadful news coming out of Germany and their sense of guilt at not being able to assist their families. One German camp leader, for example, offered to give up fifty percent of his own rations if they could be delivered to starving children in Germany. It was in response to this desperate situation that we were able to develop one of our more dramatic programs. In spite of low wages, men were desperately trying to save funds in order to send them to their families with our assistance, but since the state of Germany did not exist, there was no way for a currency exchange program to be set up.

It is a long and frenetic story, but, in brief, we were able to establish in cooperation with the Belgian officials and occupying powers a food and clothing parcel program which made it possible for prisoners to buy out of their small incomes food and clothing. With a labeled address written in their own hand, we then delivered these parcels by truck to Köln and put them in the POW post for delivery to the homes of the prisoners. This turned out to be a very successful program and had a great effect on the morale of the laborers themselves, as well as being very often the margin of subsistence for their families in Germany.

This experience articulated for us a cardinal principle which was to inform our whole approach thereafter. The fact that men, though interned, could by their own labor provide assistance to distressed families and had the ability to address parcel labels by their own hands, contributed to a decent self-respect which had a remarkable multiplying effect on the attitude of the POW's and the extent of services made possible. Not only did coal production increase, which pleased the Belgian authorities no end, but the contributions of labor, talent, and money willingly made, extended both the quality and quantity of services and the length of time in a period of shrinking budget.

In March, 1947, I was sent to Germany as director of the World's YMCA services to POW's. In many ways it was a logical third step in our planned development, and there I was to be joined by Delmar Wedel and Ernest Lefever and by several returnees, men whom we had known over a period of three to eight years. In reflection, this last service was perhaps the most important. It achieved particular significance by being done largely by our own POW alumni who joined in a common effort to serve the returnees.

Work With Prisoners of War

It was one thing for British and Americans, for example, to return to their own victorious and relatively stable societies. It was quite another for repatriates to return to a nation that no longer existed. Every major city was destroyed. Some 12,000,000 refugees had fled from the east or were driven from their homes which were now occupied by other nationalities. Over 1,000,000 other persons were homeless, living in camps or in other ways representing roving populations. Another 1,000,000 non-German DP's could not return to their own lands; their resettlement was largely dependent on their economic worth to the countries willing to accept them. Add to that 6,000,000 returnees from twenty-six countries of the world and you have a situation rife with skepticism, nihilism, and chauvinism. But now you take a population where existence itself is suffering and add to that the Nuremberg indictment— an indictment of war guilt for a whole population. Not only were war criminals *per se* indicted and incarcerated at places like Fischbecke, Dachau, and Augsburg, but hundreds of thousands of Germans were interned under a general indictment awaiting the results of so-called *Spruchkammer* (de-Nazification) proceedings.

A list of the services performed by our organization would fill a page, but our main interest, once again, was in the POW's who were returning at the rate of 50,000 to 100,000 per month through nine discharge centers in the three western zones. By the spring of 1949 approximately 6,000,000 had come home. For more than three years two small rural communities were perhaps the most important communities in Germany. Munsterlager, deep in the Lüneburger Heide, and Friedland, on the border of the Russian and British zones, were the sites of the oldest and largest discharge centers for POW's.

Here a picture is worth a thousand words. After a half million returning POW's have passed through on trains and dropped at the station, the local German citizen has become accustomed to a familiar figure. By a passing glance he can tell if the POW is returning from the north, south, east, or west. As a chalk-marked train pulls into the siding with inscriptions such as "We've come home to Mother," or "We have come from Bdein Sheik Addel Kabar," and shouting men emerge, with suntanned faces weighed down with the burden of their luggage and contraband, he smiles. Here are men returning physically strong with a wealth of material, but what is more important, unbroken spirits. However, the local citizen smiles rather ruefully when he thinks of the disillusionment these men will undergo in the coming weeks.

Sixty miles away another train from the opposite direction comes in to a siding. These men too are standing at the window gazing listlessly at this, another point of transit. Seldom does the local citizen see a waving hand or hear a shout. Undoubtedly they are enjoying an inner happiness but it would defy the sharpest observer to detect it on the expressionless and haggard faces. As they leave the train they stare as if unable to comprehend the world about them.

This returnee is greeted by another sight. Thousands of men missing in eastern campaigns were being sought by relatives. So the returnee was greeted by women holding pictures of their missing husbands asking if any of the returnees had information of their whereabouts. Our bulletin boards at Munsterlager and Friedland were filled with notices inquiring about missing soldiers. For three years we had been almost incidentally conducting a tracing service which became a major part of our program with upwards of 10,000 names for whom information was being sought.

WPA was never thought of as a relief agency. Yet it was impossible to overlook the desperate need for food and clothing and medical care among returnees from the east during this period. The Russian definition of an able-bodied man was one who could take two steps. My diary shows that out of one transport, for example, of 651 men, 525 had immediately to be hospitalized. Clothing distribution was done by stringent standards and dictated that a man must be (1) a homeless refugee and (2) his clothing unfit for wear until he reached his destination. Even so, during one month we clothed 2,000 men.

Most of those returnees wore a uniform issued five to eight years before in which they had worked and slept since the day of capture. Shoes, if indeed they wore them at all, usually consisted only of wooden slabs with canvas uppers. In an effort to assist in health programs, we set up a system of some twenty rest centers where men could be assigned for a period as long as six weeks. There the diet consisted of 1,200 calories but in case after case the men gained from twelve to twenty pounds during that period.

Work With Prisoners of War

That program, feeble as it may have been, was one of our most important activities. However, we were generally oriented to preparing the returnee for and assisting him in re-assimilation into his home community. Ideally this was a task to be performed by German organizations and German communities. But there was no escaping the fact that the World's YMCA, because of its international character, enjoyed a neutral position in the internal struggle with communal institutions which made it possible for us to be of great assistance as a catalytic agency. We, therefore, worked to the best of our ability to place these trained men in established German institutions to assist in their reconstruction for continued service to the German community.

This was a principle we applied to ourselves as well. I could leave Germany in March, 1949, in the sure confidence that the work would be carried on and its future shaped by competent hands. I would like to call that roll but time and memory fail me in part. There was Werner Lott, U-boat captain captured by Lord Mountbatten in October 1939, seven years a POW in England and Canada, my successor in Germany and today head of a multi-million dollar rehabilitation program in Germany jointly sponsored by the German government and the German YMCA. There was Leberecht von Viebahn, scion of a prominent Junker family of farmers, theologians, and generals, who lost everything but a tractor during the war, and who once reported in the dire winter of 1946 that he had spent 600 hours on trains and 600 hours waiting for trains, and meekly requested that a Volkswagen would greatly assist his work! There was Eric Hoffmann, a young POW from Hamburg, later a student and graduate of Manchester College, now a member of a research organization in Washington, D. C. These men span the generations, middle age, old, and young, whose world was drastically altered.

What more can I say? These have been the recollections of one man on his used past. Many who were involved will have different memories and so it should be. In reflection it is the story of a process which developed as though by its own inner logic and as though historical events determined their own meaning. It was a process informed by a natural piety of self-respect and mutual respect so that no man was subservient to another. It was a process carried on by men of integrity and humility with a passion for ultimate values. For nearly a decade WPA moved from place to place like Abraham, established itself in tents as though forever, yet was prepared to move on with twenty-four hours' notice. In many ways we were aliens in strange lands, not to settle there, but to assist in the resettlement of those who had lost the past. In short, we were to work ourselves out of a job and let it be assumed by those to whom the future belonged. This we did.

7. The Heifer Project

by Thurl Metzger

The **Heifer Project** was conceived in the mind of Dan
West. As a young man, Dan made a personal vow to
sacrifice as much for peace as a soldier does for war. His mission took him to Spain where, under the auspices of AFSC, he
did relief work during the Spanish Civil War. A part of his
work, as Dan described it, was to distribute limited supplies of
powdered milk to war orphans. There was never enough for all,
so they were compelled to make decisions as to which babies
had the best chance of survival and the milk was rationed to
them. It occurred to Dan that dairy heifers should be brought
to Spain as quickly as possible to replace the stock that was
destroyed by war.

When Dan returned to his home near Goshen, Indiana, he
discussed the idea with his neighbors, then formed the first
"Heifers for Relief" committee in 1939. The members were O.
W. Stine, farmer and accountant; Virgil Mock, farmer; Abe
Neff, farmer; George Craig, farmer; Ivan Syler, elevator
operator; John Metzler, district secretary for Northern Indiana,
Church of the Brethren; and Dan West, who served continuously with the organization until his death in 1971. The
first calf donated to the program was raised by Claire Stine,
son of the original chairman.

The following year the program was adopted by the
Northern Indiana District of the Church of the Brethren, but
interest and support had already spread far beyond district
lines. The beginning was an act of faith for no one knew how
the animals would be delivered overseas. By the time the heifers
were mature and ready to be shipped, World War II had
broken out and there was no possibility of shipping heifers to
Spain. Some were shipped to sharecroppers in southern USA,
and others to the Brethren service project in Puerto Rico.

The idea continued to spread through Brethren communities in Indiana, Ohio, Pennsylvania, Maryland, Virginia,

and west through Illinois and Iowa to California, so that by the end of World War II there were hundreds of "heifers for relief." In the meantime BSC, under the chairmanship of Dr. Andrew Cordier, with M. R. Zigler as executive secretary, adopted Heifer Project as an official Brethren Service program and employed Benjamin Bushong, a dairy farmer and businessman from Lancaster County, Pennsylvania, as the first executive secretary. An office was opened at the newly acquired Brethren Service Center at New Windsor, Maryland.

UNRRA, established at the cessation of hostilities, made immediate arrangements to transport "relief heifers" and also developed a livestock program of its own. Initial shipments went to France and Belgium, followed by numerous shipments to all of the Eastern European countries and to Greece and Italy. Brethren Service not only provided attendants for their shipments, but served as a recruiting agent for UNRRA livestock shipments, and the term "seagoing cowboy" was born.

The alumni of that group number in the thousands, including ministers, teachers, farmers, and laborers from nearly every community in the country. The cattle came in by thousands; and so the farm of Roger Roop, near Union Bridge, Maryland, was rented as a holding center, and Roger was employed as manager. From there they were shipped to piers at Baltimore, Newport News, and Atlanta, to be loaded aboard ships. Subsequently additional centers were established in Ohio, Indiana, and Wisconsin to regulate cattle movement.

Though the program operated under the corporation of BSC, other organizations joined the reconstituted Heifer Project Committee during the decade of the 1940s. Among these were the Evangelical and Reformed World Service Committee, the Home Mission Society of the Northern Baptist Convention, MCC, the National Catholic Rural Life Society, and the Rural Life Association. It was not until 1953 that Heifer Project was incorporated as an independent, nonprofit organization.

The UNRRA program was terminated rather abruptly in 1947, leaving hundreds of donated cattle in Heifer Project holding centers. As there was no means of delivering them to Europe some were sold and it seemed that the program would end. Shipments continued to be made as transportation funds could be procured from other sources.

The Heifer Project

Thurl Metzger was employed as executive director in 1952 and soon thereafter was invited by the United Nations Korean Reconstruction Agency to survey livestock needs in Korea. As a result, three plane loads of hatching eggs were sent to Korea and the program moved from relief to rehabilitation and development.

Another significant program opportunity occurred in Germany. It will be recalled that as a result of the Yalta and Potsdam agreements the Eastern European countries were permitted to expel all people of German descent. Some twelve million people were compelled to leave their homesteads, with only what they could carry with them, and migrate to refugee camps in Germany. It is to the credit of the postwar West German government that immediate plans were made to handle the refugee problem. A ministry was created at cabinet level and an additional tax was assessed for refugee resettlement. Land was purchased and homes were built and sold to refugee farmers on long-term, low-interest loans. Heifer Project was invited to assist this group, and for a period of eight years sent shipments from fifty to sixty-five animals at six-week intervals, using the center hold of the ship known to hundreds of "seagoing cowboys" as the *S. S. American Importer.*

A new processing center was established on the farm of Jerry Cassel, and shipments were managed by Rev. Milton Hershey of Manheim, Pennsylvania. Milton Hershey accompanied each shipment to the port of embarkation in New York, and it was always amazing to see the reception he was given by longshoremen who were neither Pennsylvanian nor Brethren in habits or speech. John Eberly, Brethren Service representative in Germany, made the initial plans for distribution and an office was established in Kassel House. The program was subsequently serviced by a series of Brethren Service volunteers including Max Snider who later, with his wife, was among those who perished in a fateful KLM crash in 1958.

As the emotions of war subsided it also became possible to develop significant projects in Japan, first with shipments of dairy goats, then with dairy cattle to pioneer communities in Hokkaido. Also, as the program became known, an increasing number of requests were received from developing nations. First among these was Ecuador, and an initial shipment was made to the Brethren Mission at Calderón under the direction

146

of Benton Rhoades. Benton later joined the staff of the Agency for International Development, and in cooperation with that agency Heifer Project entered into a national livestock improvement program. A part of that development was the leasing of a farm in Santo Domingo de los Colorados, owned by the Brethren, and transforming it into a national reproduction and training center and stocking it with both beef and dairy cattle.

Among the historic events of that period was a shipment of cattle to the Soviet Union in 1956. The shipment was accompanied by Mark Schrock and Milo Yoder of Goshen, Indiana, and Paul Miller of Waterloo, Iowa. Thurl Metzger joined them on arrival in Russia, as guest of the Ministry of Agriculture. Though this was a period of political tension we were graciously received with genuine hospitality, giving credence to M. R. Zigler's frequent statement that "... you can go anywhere on the back of a heifer...."

As mentioned previously the program was incorporated as a separate organization in 1953. Membership currently includes eleven religious bodies as member agencies and four associate agencies.

The office has been moved from New Windsor, Maryland, to North Manchester, Indiana, to Upper Darby, Pennsylvania, to St. Louis, Missouri, to Little Rock, Arkansas—and both the overseas and domestic staff have been enlarged. The program has changed from relief to rehabilitation to development, requiring new procedures and techniques. But the purpose is the same as that originally conceived by Dan West and implemented by the first committee, which is to help those in need regardless of race, creed, or politics and in a way that will permit them to share the increase.

8. The CROP Idea

by John D. Metzler, Sr.

Patiently, but maybe not happily, the oxen yoked to the cart stood with large snowflakes drifting down on them, on the bushes, and on the surroundings while "Abraham Lincoln" carried a bag of flour from his store to the cart to begin its journey overseas to feed hungry people. Photographers and radio announcers recorded the plodding movement of the loaded cart through the snow as the beginning of one section of the Abraham Lincoln Friendship Train. Goods from the Springfield State Park Lincoln store moved from that store by ox cart, then by truck, finishing the trip through the Springfield streets by ox cart to the train.

At the same time the governor of Nebraska, suitably dressed with brakeman's cap and striped denim jacket, took part in a dedication ceremony. In Lincoln, carloads of Nebraska-produced foodstuffs in the train standing on the mainline in front of the passenger station waited the time to move. At the proper moment the governor mounted the ladder on the side of a car, leaned out so that the engineer could see him, and gave the highball signal. This section of the Abraham Lincoln Friendship Train started moving toward its rendezvous with the food from Lincoln's store, to be shipped to Europe as a gift from the heart of midwest rural America to Europe's hungry. The date was Lincoln's birthday, 1948.

It was late in the preceding year that the Southwest Special Friendship Train, all made up, had stood on the elevated tracks in Wichita. Church and civic representatives, along with massed high school bands and choruses on the street below participated in the presentation and dedication of the trainload of wheat. Columnist Drew Pearson, the president of the railroad, and a CROP representative on the rear platform of the train accepted the gift. While the massed choir sang, the train slowly began rolling eastward on its way to port. Traveling only by daylight until near Chicago, the train was met at crossroads by children dismissed from school to take part in the celebration. At railroad stations in towns, communities added carloads of wheat as their gift to the outpouring of America. At one stop a group of Indians in ceremonial costume waited, and an Indian boy and girl mounted to the rear platform to present a symbolic gift of ears of Indian corn in a handwoven basket.

As the train approached Chicago, excitement increased. Drew Pearson's radio broadcasts and newspaper bulletins had kept people informed of the progress of the train and contributions to it. With airplanes flying overhead to photograph and report on the train, with searchlights playing from a special car near the head of the train, Chicago was reached where again participatory ceremonies were held.

There was drama in the CROP idea; drama as CROP participated with Drew Pearson Friendship Trains, both that one starting in California and the Southwest Special; drama with the Abraham Lincoln Friendship Trains; drama as "Friendships" were loaded at the Chicago port; drama as dedications were held from huge trucks in vast wheatfields, in railroad yards, at church conventions, at the Assembly of the National Council of Churches; drama at the Mountain of Wheat in Montana. Rural America was welcoming this opportunity to ease its conscience by sharing its abundance of food with the hungry sufferers from the war that had brought riches to the United States.

The application may have been new, but the idea of direct sharing of the products of one's own work where there is need was not new to Brethren.

From barn raisings, to direct giving and transporting of food to men in CPS camps, to community pooling of food in CROP campaigns, the basic idea is one. Somehow one's crops are an extension of one's own self. There is a difference between giving actual produce resulting from the partnership of God and man working the soil, and selling that crop and writing a check on the cash received. It not only eliminates the middle man but seems to be a much more personal involvement.

With a truck network distributing homegrown and processed food to CPS men, it was logical to collect clothing for relief. With this experience, it was a short step to handling railroad cars of grain, giving them to the Netherlands Purchasing Commission for shipping to Holland, the first country to which transportation was available following the war. Carloads of wheat from many states, midwest, southwest, northwest, were handled by the Material Aid Department of Brethren Service. A telephone call relayed from Moundridge, Kansas, asked if a gift of flour, mostly from Mennonite farmers of that community, could be handled. Negotiations resulted in nineteen carloads of flour moving from Moundridge through BSC and CWS channels to Europe. Perhaps fifty carloads were handled in all just for the Netherlands.

The next question was posed by M. R. Zigler on behalf of and to Brethren Service: "If Brethren, Mennonite, and Evangelical and Reformed farmers will give carloads of foodstuffs directly to relief of hunger, will other Christians respond to such an opportunity?"

So it was that in April, 1947, we made a quick trip to visit councils of churches in various wheat-producing areas to ask about probable response and cooperation. With uniformly favorable replies our next steps in the exploration included interviews with the executive of the President's Control Board (later Advisory Board) for Voluntary Foreign Aid; with the head of the USDA Extension Service ("America must do this to save its own soul"); with the staff of CWS ("O.K. if you don't ask us to handle carloads of corn in our office, because we can't put it under our desks"); with the assistant to the Secretary General of the United Nations ("Stay close to the churches"). During this time the gifts of carloads of grain continued to be handled through the New Windsor BSC office in close cooperation with CWS. Thrills were numerous, as when a single small Illinois congregation contributed an entire carload of grain and the pastor was so filled with emotion he found it difficult to speak to ask for shipping instructions.

In June, 1947, BSC and the World Service Commission of the Evangelical and Reformed church each put $5,000 into a fund and employed a field worker, A. N. Lambert. He was told to start organizing, working with state councils of churches, and through the New Windsor office, even though there was no name and no assurance that CWS could be geared to handle such a program. Catholic Relief Service was asked if they would be interested in such a program, as was Lutheran World

Relief. Because harvest was taking place and nature would not stop for churchly negotiations, CWS agreed to sponsor the idea with the understanding that the invitation was open for joint participation with other agencies. At a conversation in the office of CWS, the name of the new activity, Christian Rural Overseas Program, was selected so that its initials would spell CROP.

So it came to pass that on August 1, 1947, CROP as an idea, with an active fieldman already working in the Southwest wheat areas, with all its files in one briefcase, came to Chicago to be nearer the midwestern agricultural areas. The material aid director for BSC, John D. Metzler, Sr., became CROP's first director. A one-room office was opened in a Bethany Seminary dormitory and business started. It was not long that one room was enough. The early activities were almost as much an emotional response as a business enterprise. There were many who volunteered to help. The Christian (Disciples of Christ) Church loaned a full-time staff person for six months to help in the field organizing. Reportedly one of the field workers never looked at the name of the food item in a restaurant menu, merely the price. His concern was to get food to the hungry; he was operating on the conviction that he would not starve on any restaurant food although he might not relish the taste.

There was effective intercommunication in the office—reports of new contributions received were shouted for all to hear and rejoice in. Many times staff workers in going from state to state would work all day, ride the train all night, and work the next day, keeping up the pace for a solid week with neither break nor time off. In the active areas thousands volunteered to help. A highly respected "dean of the elevator owners" of Kansas used the telephone so successfully that there were ninety-nine carloads of wheat given for transport on the Southwest Special Friendship Train.

Negotiations with other religious groups were continuing, and a plan was worked out so that the National Catholic Rural Life Conference, acting as agent for Catholic Relief Service, became a sponsoring agency. Lutheran World Relief named a representative to the directing cabinet of CROP. Jewish agencies were invited to become an active partner but declined because of the small number of Jewish farmers. Up to that time, this was probably the most successful demonstration in modern times that major religious groups could cooperate in such an approach to community action. Later a citation was awarded CROP during National Brotherhood Week. The plan adopted made arrangements for the donor to designate the agency which he wanted to handle his gift and arrange for its distribution overseas. CROP received and transmitted contributions for any designated agency, whether that agency was a partner in the management of CROP or not.

When Drew Pearson received a request to organize and sponsor a Friendship Train to help the hungry of Europe, the idea appealed to him, but he did not have the organization nor facilities for handling such commodities. After negotiations, CROP became an advisor and assistant in arranging shipment, and through parent agencies, delivery and distribution of the goods overseas. This experience and publicity, a generally happy arrangement, gave a start that would have been more slowly achieved without Mr. Pearson's name, support, and media facilities.

Success was remarkable, especially during the first few years when the overseas needs were so great. Shipments of food from the West Coast went mostly to Japan. Europe received shipments from the Gulf, East Coast, and Great Lakes ports. Thousands of tons—whole shiploads—of wheat went to Germany and enabled some German flour mills to begin work again. Because CROP was inclusive religiously, cooperatives, milling and processing firms, elevators and grain companies could and did contribute.

Reports coming back through church channels told of the distribution on the basis of need, and the areas of contribution increased. Not only wheat, but corn, rice, cotton, peanuts, dried fruits, and other products were shipped. Agricultural firms made agreements to receive some commodities not suitable for direct shipment and transferred them under favorable terms into goods suitable for shipment. Dairy cooperatives arranged to set aside fluid milk by members, and powdered milk was shipped. In a similar way various commodities—relief cereal, lard, fats, canned meats, syrup, sugar, oil—were among foods provided through CROP for shipment by the parent agencies.

After the first highly emotional response to need was past, the cost of a threefold religious approach to the community and its integration and coordination there proved to be too costly. It was then decided that CWS would continue as the sponsor-director of CROP, and that donors could designate the agency of their choice. Since 1952 CROP has been operated on this basis by CWS. It has been a channel for giving by and to agencies and groups widely different, ranging from Four Square Gospel, to Salvation Army, to National Association of Evangelicals, to Catholic Relief Services, to Lutheran World Relief, to Mennonites, to CWS and others.

CROP with its church-sponsored community program has remained with its basic appeal—to help those in need overseas. As needs and opportunities have changed, the response has changed from the immediate lifesaving food to means for food production—seed, tools, fertilizers, irrigation projects, or whatever may be required to help the overseas community to move toward providing for its own needs. Areas in the world have shifted: from Western Europe, to the rest of Europe, Japan, Africa, Latin America. With CWS responsible for planning of distribution, and relying on local agencies in the country of receipt, overall efficiency is high.

There is no accurate way to compute the value of the contributions through CROP. While actual cash market value of contributed goods, handling charges, contributed freight—both internal rail freight and ocean freight—totals into the millions of dollars, it is impossible to calculate and add the value of free tariff entry and internal handling for recipient countries, plus administrative management, plus the greater values achieved there. No way is known to set a value on human life. Then consider, for example, the thousands of acres of corn grown from CROP-donated seed. The benefits of school gardens from contributed vegetable seed is literally incalculable. Who can tell the real value of an irrigation project over the years, or the benefit of a pure-water well for a village?

The expressions of gratitude from overseas partners have been numerous and varied. The Netherlands was one of the first countries to say, "Thank you, we can make out on our own now. Please send the gifts to more needy areas." France planned a *Merci* train, sending some twenty of their smaller railroad cars loaded with suitable gifts of gratitude to be given to major areas of the United States. They were distributed, again by special trains retracing the route of the original

Friendship Trains. Children of Germany were challenged to give their *pfennige* to help others "as the children of the United States did." Many handmade gifts from many countries, letters of thanks, essays (sometimes highly fanciful) from school children came to CROP. As the economies of Western European nations improved, those countries became and remained major sources of help for other needy areas.

CROP's emphasis on community, its dependence on local church cooperation, its emphasis on bulk rather than package generosity, its practicality in appealing for commodities which could be shipped directly to meet need, its adaptation of response to changing needs and changing areas—all have contributed to the continuance and success of the CROP idea.

9. The UNRRA Brethren Service Unit

by Howard E. Sollenberger

With the end of World War II, BSC was seeking ways in which young men could demonstrate their humanitarian concerns for people who had suffered the ravages of war. After many years of missionary work in China, the operation of a relief program in the region of southeast Shansi Province during the early years of the Japan-China conflict, continuing relief work in Free China during the war, and an unsuccessful effort to send a medical unit to China under the CPS program, it was natural that there should be a special interest in China.

Information gathered by the UNRRA office in China in the spring of 1946 revealed that the food situation in that country was critically growing worse. An estimated thirty-three million persons were existing on an inadequate diet, with seven million on the brink of starvation. Honan Province was most seriously affected by the impending famine. Flooding caused by a break in the Yellow River dykes had taken two million of China's most fertile acres out of production. The provinces of Hunan, Anhwei, Kiangsi Fukien, Shansi, and Shantung were also facing famine conditions resulting from military campaigns, loss of food production, and the disruption of transportation.

The Chinese government with the help of UNRRA engineers was planning a major emergency effort to close the mile-long main break in the dykes of the Yellow River by July, 1946, so late crops could be planted, thereby providing immediate food from agricultural land returned to production. Two thousand tractors had been requested from UNRRA to speed up the process of land reclamation. Western technicians who would be willing to go into these devastated areas with farm machinery to train Chinese operators and maintenance crews and to supervise operations were essential to the program since the Chinese themselves had no experience in mechanized farming.

The UNRRA Brethren Service Unit

When BSC was approached by the Chinese government for assistance they responded immediately. A planning committee composed of Cheng Pao-nan, of the Chinese National Reconstruction and Rehabilitation Administration (CNRRA); Andrew Cordova, Agricultural Rehabilitation Division (AGREHAB) of UNRRA; Raymond Hall, Office of Far Eastern Affairs, UNRRA; M. R. Zigler, BSC; and Howard Sollenberger, of the UNRRA Training Office, was established to work out the details of a project. A formal agreement between UNRRA and BSC was signed on July 15, 1946, setting up what was to be called the UNRRA Brethren Service Unit (BSU).

The agreement provided that BSC recruit fifty volunteers with farm and/or mechanical experience for preliminary technical training in the use and maintenance of the equipment being shipped to China. These volunteers would serve without salary, but would be treated as UNRRA employees with all privileges, immunities, and responsibilities provided regular employees. UNRRA would provide necessary processing, expenses related to training, transportation to and from China, and allowances for personal effects.

CNRRA, in addition to providing local currency funding for operating projects, would assume responsibilities for maintaining the unit while in China. This included living facilities, an allowance for food, all transportation within China, necessary personal services and incidental Chinese currency expenses on the same basis as for regular UNRRA personnel.

Howard Sollenberger was appointed to represent BSC as director of the unit and to serve as liaison officer with UNRRA and CNRRA. Additional administrative personnel were to be provided in China by the Agricultural Rehabilitation Division of UNRRA. Personnel administration of the unit was to be under BSC with operational supervision assigned to CNRRA.

To clarify the position of BSC with regard to the utilization of the unit, Leland Brubaker sent a communication to UNRRA officials. The letter emphasized the tradition of political neutrality of BSC and the desire to aid all factions of the Chinese people.

The BSC recruitment effort was started in May, 1946, in anticipation of the agreement. The search for volunteers was not limited to members of the Church of the Brethren, or even to members of the historic peace churches. A very concerted effort was made to avoid glamorizing the operation and to discourage adventure seekers. In early recruitment bulletins some of the anticipated problems and rigorous conditions of living and working in China were clearly put to the applicants.

Recruitment under way, arrangements were made for technical training in the use, maintenance, and repair of equipment with four agricultural machinery companies. The first group of fourteen recruits reported on July 18, 1946, for two weeks of intensive training at the International Harvester Company. Approximately two thirds of this group had farm-background experience, others had a knowledge of Chinese or some administrative qualification which was felt would be helpful in carrying out the mission in China. Only one of the men was a trained, experienced mechanic. Efforts were also made to organize an orientation program on China and to start Chinese language study. The apparent urgency in getting the men to China made any systematic training impossible even though this was strongly recommended.

Howard Sollenberger and the first member of the unit, Forest Whitcher, left for Shanghai in the latter part of August to make arrangements for the arrival of the first group. Immediately problems, both foreseen and unforeseen, became apparent. In spite of the urgent call for personnel, preparations for their utilization in field operations were considerably behind schedule. Warehousing and assembly facilities in Shanghai were still in the planning stage and there was no definite information regarding the arrival of tractors and equipment. The army surplus equipment that was already in China was mostly inoperable and without equipment or spare parts.

When the first contingent of the unit arrived in mid-September they were immediately put to work clearing the wharf. Literally with only pliers, wrenches, and screwdrivers they went to work putting bulldozers and I-9 tractors in running condition so that they could be moved or used in clearing the congested wharf. Later unit members helped establish the assembly and repair center at Point Island. Owing to continued delays in procuring equipment and incomplete arrangements for the utilization of more volunteers, BSC was advised to delay recruitment. As it worked out, the unit did not reach its full strength of fifty until February, 1947.

The UNRRA Brethren Service Unit

Darwin Solomon was the first BSU man to be sent to the field. He was initially attached to a small team of Mennonite volunteers who were already working in the Yellow River-flooded region of Honan Province, but was also to prepare the way for the first BSU contingent. Part of the preparation in which BSU volunteers were subsequently involved was the establishment of a central supply and service depot at Lo Ho, a small town on the Ping-Han railway. In late October, 1946, Harvey Accola, Raymond Hoff and Oliver Eckles arrived with twelve tractors and began to train student operators. This was the beginning of the largest and most complex operation undertaken by the BSU. In the process of training twenty-seven students, this unit plowed the first land—some eight hundred acres near the village of Fang Ch'eng.

The Fang Ch'eng training project completed, the operation moved to Lien Sze, which was to be developed as the hub of the northern flooded area tractor operations. Seventy tractors were eventually put into operation under the supervision of nine BSU members; 18,000 acres were plowed and planted in kaoliang, soy beans, and sweet potatoes. CNRRA planned to organize a large cooperative involving fifty villages with Lien Sze as its center. It seemed that operations in Yellow River-flooded area were finally getting under way. But in May, 1947, military activities between the Nationalists and the Communists broke out and the town changed hands six times in ten days. Later the Nationalists began fortifying the project compound.

A plowing project at Wang P'ai Fen, the southern hub of the flooded area, was opened in March, 1946. Despite many difficulties BSU personnel reported that an estimated 6,540 acres had been plowed and mostly planted after three months. As a result of the stimulus of the plowing project, villages and roads were being rebuilt and many refugees were returning. The Wang P'ai Fen project was short-lived. It had to be evacuated on July 22 because of military activities in the area.

The so-called "Panco" project at Cheng Chiao, set up by Bob Pannebecker and Dave Cole, was the first to be established in territory that was definitely Communist-controlled. They reported problems in clearing the land for plowing, late arrival of students, and absence of Communist authorities.

On numerous occasions personnel moving in and out of

the Communist-controlled areas were fired on by both sides. Vehicles were stopped at gunpoint and commandeered for military purposes. The area became so unstable that in July an evacuation of BSU personnel from the contested area was ordered. During the evacuation four members were captured and held for three days.

At a meeting of the Honan contingent of BSU with M. R. Zigler, who was visiting operations for BSC, it was agreed that regular operations could not continue in an environment of active civil war. It was subsequently decided that BSU participation in the Honan operations should be phased out. At that time the Yellow River-flooded area projects involved seventeen BSU personnel. Five were assigned to the Maintenance Center at Lo Ho, ten to field operation, one to administrative support, and one to seed purchasing. Some 35,000 acres of land had been brought back into cultivation and 340 Chinese had been trained to operate and maintain farm machinery. These accomplishments were far short of the original objectives but were nonetheless a significant achievement considering the instability of the area and other factors over which BSU had no control.

While operations in the contested areas of Honan were short-lived, it was felt that efforts should be made to set up a project in an area where Communist control was not contested, to demonstrate the neutrality of BSU operations. Shantung was selected as a possible area. However, it was not until April, 1947, that forty tractors with farming equipment were released for the Communist area. Three BSU men accompanied the shipment, which was unloaded at Chefoo for transshipment to an operational site. Unexplained delays held the equipment in Chefoo for six weeks during which time a training school was held for thirty students. During June the forty tractors were transshipped to Yang Chiao Kou and convoyed by the BSU men three hundred miles overland to a project site near Lin Ching, traveling at easy stages, mostly in the early mornings and evenings, to avoid bombing and strafing by Nationalist planes.

The land reclamation area selected by the Communist authorities consisted of approximately 100,000 acreas of good flat sandy soil. Differences of opinion over whether the equipment should be kept together and operated as a single unit or disbursed to a number of smaller projects again held up operations. The BSU men objected to dispersal of the equipment during the initial training period on the grounds of lack of experienced operators and maintenance men. Even though verbal agreement was reached on this issue, local CLARA (Communist counterpart of CNRRA) officials refused to release the equipment. Mr. Thomfordo of UNRRA and William Hinton, a BSU volunteer, were sent up from Shanghai to replace the original BSU team and to negotiate arrangements for putting the equipment into operation. They were later joined by Raymond Hoff, also of BSU. Forty additional students were finally trained and 1,665 acres plowed before the gas supply ran out.

The Hupeh project was established 110 miles west of Hankow in an area devastated by the Japanese scorched-earth policy. The first plowing was to return a former Japanese airfield to cultivation. Eight BSU men with one hundred tractors were at various times working in this area. One of the problems was how to plow land covered with eighteen-foot-high reeds. A successful powercutter attached to a tractor was designed by Gordon Brand and George Snyder to solve the problem. A side interest at the project was the establishment, by the BSU men, of an outpatient clinic which treated up to twenty-five patients per day. Hupeh was one of the more successful projects. The supervisory relationship of BSU through the UNRRA AGREHAB officer was excellent. BSU members were given considerable responsibility and support in the field and proved capable of handling operations.

Manchuria had from the beginning been considered as a site for major tractor operations. Two hundred tractors and nine BSU men had been scheduled for this area. The first shipment left Shanghai in May escorted by an UNRRA tractor maintenance superintendent and one BSU man, Ralph Soelzer. The ship went aground off the Shantung coast and was considered "bounty of war" by the Communists, who controlled that section of the coastline. Soelzer and the UNRRA representative were held as prisoners for six weeks. Additional equipment, accompanied by BSU volunteers, was eventually shipped to Mukden, where Franklin Wallick, Dale Williams, Ivan Patterson, and Lester Brumbaugh carried out a training program. By that time civil war had erupted in Manchuria, severely limiting the possibility of operations. After training a group of sixty students, the BSU men were withdrawn.

While BSU had felt that its activities should be concentrated in a few major land reclamation and food-production projects, political pressure resulted in the scattering of small projects from Kwangtung in the south to Manchuria in the north, and from Formosa off the southeast coast to Suiyuan in the northwest. Relatively minor operations were attempted in such scattered areas as Hupeh, Kiangsu, Anhwei, Kwangsi, Chekiang, Hunan, Sui-Yuan, Formosa, and Kwangtung Provinces. Some limited successes were achieved but a variety of problems were faced. The Sui-Yuan project was closed after plowing only 1,400 acres owing to lack of CNRRA financial support and a shortage of gas and oil. The equipment destined for Formosa was shipwrecked, but the accompanying BSU volunteer, Lester Brumbaugh, was rescued. Projects in Anhwei, Kwangtung, and Hunan were flooded out.

There were occasions when members of BSU were not fully utilized in tractor projects. Rather than waiting for equipment to arrive or for arrangements to be made by CNRRA, they volunteered for other useful work. These activities included wharf clearances, expediting shipments of UNRRA equipment and supplies to the provinces, warehousing, well drilling, distribution of cattle sent to China by BSC, and field distribution of UNRRA supplies. Several of the men were also assigned at various times to assist in setting up small agricultural industries. Various members undertook community service projects in Shanghai or at their project sites.

M. R. Zigler, executive secretary of BSC, was sent to China by UNRRA to observe the utilization and work of BSU during July, 1947. Apart from observing the immediate work of the unit, he was concerned about the problems of maintaining a position of neutrality while working under the supervision of CNRRA, an arm of the Nationalist government. He was also interested in planning for post-UNRRA work in China. During his visit, Zigler visited operations in Honan, Hupeh, Kiangsi, Hunan, and attended a conference of BSU in Hangchow and a joint Brethren Mission-BSC conference in Peking.

The Hangchow conference, in addition to reviewing operations of BSU, considered the problem of voluntary agency personnel working under an international organization, discussed the difficulties of working in an area torn by civil war, and submitted recommendations on an extended agreement with UNRRA.

UNRRA had requested that there be an extension of the agreement through December 31, 1947. The conference accepted this proposal, with certain stipulations, stating: "In spite of the many obstacles that have been listed and the frequent variances of the program from the paramount aim which have hindered and obstructed efficient operations; we nonetheless feel that if certain specified conditions which we will list are met to facilitate the most efficient operations, we of the BSU desire to continue food production as our number one objective for the remainder of the UNRRA period."

In another resolution, BSU personnel reaffirmed their basic belief in political neutrality for relief operations and urged that ways be sought to implement this position on "both Nationalist and Communist territory in ways directly serving the needs of the common people."

An extended agreement was signed continuing BSU services on an individual voluntary basis through December 31, 1947. Howard Sollenberger left the unit in August to take a position with the Department of State in Peking, and Wendell Flory, a member of the Brethren Mission, was appointed as the post-UNRRA director of Brethren Service activities in China. Some members of the unit chose to return to the United States at the end of the one-year agreement while others stayed on through the period of the extended agreement.

An evaluation of a project such as the UNRRA Brethren Service Unit is at best difficult. Certainly a number of lessons were learned. There were a number of factors, some foreseen and some not, which limited the achievement of objectives. These included: the short life of UNRRA/CNRRA operations and their shortcomings in carrying out plans; the inexperience of Chinese farmers with machinery; the continued civil war; the inexperience of the BSU personnel.

Given these problems, the actual reclamation of some 50,000 acres of land (100,000 acres by CNRRA estimates), the training of 660 tractor operators, and other contributions made by the unit amounted to no small achievement. In fact, the accomplishments corresponded favorably with those of other

UNRRA/CNRRA operating units which were faced with many of the same problems. BSU did distinguish itself within the total spectrum of operations in China by getting out into the field where the job was to be done, rather than operating out of offices in Shanghai or in regional or provincial head-quarters.

The training of Chinese personnel in the use of farm machinery and in modern forms of administration, organization, and operations was probably as significant a contribution as the actual physical accomplishments of land reclamation. A new technological seed was planted which germinated slowly and has not yet reached maturity. There are now semi-mechanized farming operations in various parts of China and a growing interest in developing machine-aided agriculture on a much more extensive scale. Some of the Chinese trained by BSU have probably continued to work in this field.

Similarly an approach to international service, utilizing units of volunteer personnel in carrying out rehabilitation and development projects under both national and international organizations, was pioneered. While the experience of BSU working with UNRRA and CNRRA showed some of the limitations and problems it did serve as an idea that evolved into the concept of the Peace Corps.

An appraisal of the UNRRA Brethren Service Unit would not be complete without some reference to what the experience meant to the individuals involved. There has been no study done on what has happened to the members of the unit, but it is clear that a significant number were sufficiently motivated by the experience to continue in service work in both the domestic and international scene. It certainly produced a group of men with a broader perspective on the problems and realities of the human condition, and it has enabled them individually to make a greater contribution to humankind than would otherwise have been the case.

The vision of men like Leland Brubaker and M. R. Zigler was sound. As a testimony of humanitarian service, the effort was worthwhile.

10. The Development of BSC in Europe

by Eldon R. Burke

It was in the late summer of 1943 that I was given leave from my position as professor of history at Ball State University to go to Philadelphia to serve as director of a research and training project for relief which was sponsored by the service committees of the Mennonites, Friends, and Brethren. Except for the representatives sent by the three agencies, the cost was to be borne by the US government as part of the CPS service program in which it was engaged as part of the war effort. In part it was an attempt to meet the demand of the men for more significant work and in part to prepare for the relief and rehabilitation activities of the agencies which they were planning for the postwar period.

Unfortunately, when Congress passed the appropriations bill, a rider was added prohibiting the use of any funds for the training of conscientious objectors for relief. Nevertheless, the three agencies were able to persuade General Lewis B. Hershey, the head of the conscription agency, to allocate a few persons to the center so that some of the preparatory work could be done. Eventually a staff of eight to ten persons was assembled for this purpose.

Before my arrival in Philadelphia, the three agencies had rented a house at 4053 Spruce Street which was to be used as the center. My wife, Cecile Burke, became the manager of the house which was used not only for our purposes, but also for visitors who might come to the city, especially as a hostel for CPS men on leave. This meant that the staff became acquainted with many men from the camps, and several were subsequently recruited for special studies which they made in their spare time. Of the permanent personnel, the Mennonites sent Dr. M. C. Lehman and John Bender, the Brethren (in addition to myself) Robert Walters, and the Quakers, Irwin Abrams. Several CPS men were also assigned from time to time for a few weeks before they were assigned to one of the camps. Their names appear in connection with some of the publications of the center.

The most ambitious project was the preparation of a casebook for the study of relief policies and methods under the leadership of Dr. Hertha Kraus of Bryn Mawr College. In addition to the persons mentioned above, Earl Garver and Allen Eister shared in the preparation of the work for publication. A second study was a booklet on Puerto Rico, the text of which was written mainly by Earl Garver and E. B. Fincher, with illustrations by John Morgan and William Schuhle. John Bender made a special study of Mennonite activities in South America which was published in a series on the Mennonite heritage. Several studies were never published, i.e., a study of the Virgin Islands and one of Bolivia by Misti Smith. Other studies initiated by the center were developed outside and published independently.

When it became apparent that my time was not to be fully used by the center (at least, M. R. Zigler thought so) he asked me to study the sources of Brethren history which might be found in the Philadelphia area. I was able to collect several items which were subsequently sent to Elgin. Another project was a study of the handling of clothing and other relief supplies through the Quaker center in Philadelphia and the Mennonite center at Akron, Pennsylvania. In this connection M. R. developed the idea that the facilities of the defunct Blue Ridge college might be used for this purpose, and for the training of relief workers. After Christmas, 1943, I was sent to New Windsor, Maryland, to work out the ways and means by which this might be accomplished.

After much negotiation and maneuvering, the property came into the possession of BSC and the work was begun. However, even before the property was owned by the Brethren, packages and other relief material began to arrive; and my wife and I went to New Windsor to begin the handling of relief supplies. Presently John Metzler, Sr., and his wife were assigned to take over and develop the work. During these same months of the winter and spring of 1944, I was frequently sent to attend meetings in New York where organizations were being formed to carry on relief activities after the war. The overall coordinating agency was known as the American Council of Voluntary Agencies for Foreign Service, and under its auspices, the various committees for the different countries were formed. Two of the best known organizations created by them were CARE and CRALOG, the agencies which did the most for German relief.

In August, 1944, my wife was asked to go to New York to manage the Japanese Relocation Center in Brooklyn which had been begun by Ralph and Mary Smeltzer. I continued to be the Brethren representative on the various relief committees which were meeting constantly during this time. I also attended meetings of a similar kind in Washington, D. C., and became a member of a special committee of NSBRO which was authorized to care for the families of men in the CPS camps or in jail who were without means to support themselves. At the same time several additional projects were developed. One of these was the shipping of Brown Swiss bulls to Greece for the implementation of an artificial breeding program under the auspices of the Near East Foundation. At this time the Brethren also became interested in the collection of heifers for rehabilitation, from which the Heifer Project was developed. In May the first shipment of heifers was made to Puerto Rico. Another project which was discussed and developed at this time was the collection of grain and other agricultural commodities from farmers for relief purposes from which CROP later evolved.

Eventually in connection with the planning and development of the relief work of the Brethren, it became necessary for someone to go to Europe to survey the situation and to arrange for the distribution of supplies. I was chosen for this work and on May 19, 1945, sailed for Europe in the last convoy of the European war. Early in the war period John Barwick had gone to London to work with the War Prisoners' Aid of the World Alliance of the YMCA. Later Luther Harshbarger had been sent to work with him. Martha Rupel, who had had experience in relief work in Spain during the Spanish Civil War, had also been sent to work with the Mennonites in a child care project in England. Thus it was hoped that gradually some experience might be acquired for the further work of the Brethren in Europe. I arrived in London on June 1 and two weeks later went to Paris to begin the actual distribution of Brethren cattle and other relief supplies.

Through the kind assistance of the YMCA I obtained

lodging in Paris in one of the very few hotels not requisitioned by the American army and with the help of American Relief for France arranged for transportation. A driver from the Friends Ambulance Service, Hamilton Mills, also served as interpreter since my French was only a reading knowledge.

My first task was to persuade the French government to pay the transportation cost on a shipment of heifers and to arrange for their distribution. This meant that the French authorities had a considerable stake in the cattle, and it was necessary to arrange for distribution through their facilities. The principle on which distribution was based was that originally urged by Dan West that this should be a means for providing milk for needy children. Through the French ministry of agriculture a plan was prepared, and through them the cattle were delivered. I visited the various homes for children, both public and church-related, either before or after the distribution was made. At this time there were no cattle given to private individuals, and later a similar method was used in Belgium. The cattle shipped to Italy were distributed entirely by the government and the Catholic church, and I was not informed of how it was done. The Polish shipments of cattle were also handled from America. It was only later in Germany that I had anything more to do with the shipping and distribution of cattle.

In order to arrange for the distribution of clothing and other relief supplies I turned to Pastor Marc Boegner of the French Protestant church and the welfare office of the French government. In connection with these agencies a plan was developed, in imitation of the Mennonites, for the care of children in a home which we would supply. Another plan was made for the support of delinquent boys who were under the French Ministry of Justice. The latter plan was adopted. A plan was also made for the care of the needy in Calais, and Charles and Ruth Webb were given the responsibility for the work.

One of the serious problems in connection with the distribution of relief supplies came from the robbery and pilferage of goods. On that account I asked the Brethren to send a couple of "Christian truck drivers," and Isaac Earhart and Roscoe Switzer came for that purpose. In Italy a project was developed initially in cooperation with the Quakers to supply building materials for villages devastated by the war. The Brethren group sent from America after some time reconsidered the project and moved to Carrara and developed a youth project which was more to their liking and with which they had considerable success. The members of the original team were Merlin Frantz, Robert Mays, Eugene Lichty, Walter Bowman, and Mark Ebersole. Jean Frantz, Joyce Mays, Eloise Lichty, and Frances Bowman later joined their husbands.

Other relief materials were given to the Waldensians, but the desire of M. R. to establish more positive relations with them was not accomplished at this time. Two additional workers arrived in France in the fall of 1945: Grace Ritchey and Lois Rupel. Grace served for some time as my secretary and assistant and aided in the preparation of reports.

Brethren work in the Low Countries began when the YMCA sent Luther Harshbarger to Brussels to open an office. Since the Brethren decided to channel all relief supplies through CWS, it was necessary for me to correlate my activities with their counterpart in the Geneva Office of WCC. Dr. S. C. Michelfelder of the Lutheran World Federation (LWF) was the chairman of the office for the distribution of relief supplies at that time. As his representative I purchased materials and vehicles for the work of the council from surplus army stocks. At the same time I shared in the responsibilities of the YMCA office in Brussels.

In Holland, in cooperation with the YMCA, a project was developed for the care of the children of pro-Germans who were interned by the Dutch government. After the children were gathered into camps, the Brethren supplied bedding, food, and clothing; the YMCA gave recreational and educational supplies. Lois Rupel was the Brethren representative for this project in Amsterdam, Margaret Watson for the YMCA. Another Brethren project was the distribution of supplies on the island of Walcheren; Cecile Burke, Martha Rupel, Isaac Earhart, and later Lois Rupel were responsible for this work. The flour from the wheat shipments, approximately eight hundred tons, was distributed in Holland through the agency of the Dutch churches.

The work in Poland began when Bruce and Clara Woods were sent to Ostroda in December, 1946, to distribute clothing, food, and medicines. The way had been prepared by cattle shipments. In 1947 Opal Stech went to the Central Agricultural College in Warsaw to assist in the establishment of a department of home economics.

In the meantime the German committee of the American Council had created CRALOG. Early in the year 1946 I was sent to Berlin as the Brethren representative. In December, 1945, I made two trips by truck to Germany to obtain books for the YMCA which could be distributed to German POW's and to deliver toys made by German prisoners to some of the devastated towns for children at Christmas. Several days after I had arrived in Berlin I was sent to Bremen to care for some shipments which were arriving at the port. This was done at my suggestion because Bremen seemed a good location from which I could continue the other activities in which I was engaged. The CRALOG organization, however, desired that someone professionally trained and experienced in shipping should be given the responsibility for this work. Unfortunately this person died by accident on his way to Germany. This made it necessary for me to remain in Bremen.

Because my knowledge of shipping was limited, I created a shipping organization which was composed of Germans who were experienced with the practices and procedures required. Each of the German recipient agencies was invited to send a representative to handle the goods designated for distribution by them through the facilities of the CRALOG office. Thus CRALOG became the cover organization for all relief goods originating in the United States distributed to Germans. As far as I know, only the goods of the Mormons were handled otherwise, and their shipments were only distributed to members of their own sect. CARE shipments were also a kind of exception since some packages were given to general welfare, but their packages were usually designated for particular individuals. Since shipping costs were less from Bremen than from Hamburg to central Germany, and because the port was operated under American Army auspices, it was decided to use Bremen as the main port of entry.

At first only a few persons were directly employed by CRALOG; later, when the Marshall Plan came into operation and shipping was defrayed from those funds, additional personnel was necessary to supervise and control our activities. From the beginning forms were devised and reports required so that it was possible to know exactly the details of the movement of goods from the time of their arrival in Bremen until the final distribution. Thus regular reports could be sent to the agencies in America which supplemented the reports of their representatives from the various parts of Germany.

As originally planned when CRALOG was organized, the bulk of the goods was distributed by the five German welfare agencies. The Mennonites, Quakers, and Brethren distributed some materials through their own personnel. Altogether during the five years of work in the Bremen CRALOG organization we handled about a hundred thousand tons valued at about sixty-five million dollars. In the five years after my leaving the office, when everything was placed in German hands, a similar quantity of supplies was received and distributed.

Because I was spending most of my time working for the agencies of CRALOG, after some months BSC decided that I should be employed full time by them. The general Brethren administration in Europe was transferred to John E. Bowman who established an office in Geneva, Switzerland. Kurt Naylor was sent as the new representative with CRALOG and located himself at Kassel. After about a year in Holland, my wife joined me in Bremen and continued to aid in the relief activities of the area until our return to America in 1951.

Another project, the development of which was shared by the Brethren, was aimed at the rehabilitation of those physically handicapped by the war. On one of my first visits to Germany, I had to wait several hours to obtain transportation to Berlin. While sitting on a bench, I was joined by a young man who had lost a leg in the war. As he told me of the misfortunes of his family and how his whole future had been blasted by the war, there arose the suggestion that possibly something could be done for unfortunates, cripples, and handicapped persons with injuries resulting from the conflict. With the support of M. R. Zigler, I was encouraged to go ahead with the project. He arranged to have some tools sent to me from America and authorized me to buy some lumber in Sweden. I also bought a few things from the surplus property administration of the American government.

In Bremen I presented my ideas to the German officials who were inclined to try to work out a shop training program with our help. Then one day an unusual proposal was presented to me by Dr. Winebrenner of the welfare branch of the military control. He offered to give us for our use a complex of buildings and grounds, which had been evacuated by the military, on condition that we use a part of it for hospital purposes. From previous conversations with M. R. and other Brethren, I knew that the Brethren did not have the means or the desire to embark on a project of this scope. On the other hand I also felt certain that the opportunity was too good to be neglected. I was certain that the Brethren would support work if someone else assumed the major responsibility, especially if it were a German agency.

With this in mind I approached Pastor Bodo Heyne who was the leader of the Protestant welfare work in Land Bremen. He agreed to organize the project which has since that time become known as the institution of *Friedehorst*. In agreement with the deaconesses institution some of the facilities were turned over to them for use as a hospital for the treatment of tubercular patients. Thus the demand was met that a hospital be established. The Bremen authorities also took some of the land and buildings for their own purposes in the care of refugees and the homeless. The remaining facilities have been used for other welfare activities.

After about a year, the management of *Friedehorst* was given to Pastor H. J. Diehl. Support was obtained not only from Brethren but also Lutheran and other sources. The original idea of retraining and rehabilitation was not lost. The name Christopher Sauer Workshops is a memorial of Brethren support. Today it is a complex of institutions. The care of the aged, the retraining and rehabilitation of misfits in society and the physically handicapped are major activities. Over eleven hundred persons are permanent or semi-permanent residents for the period of their training. Hundreds have shared in the benefits of *Friedehorst* to date.

I remained five years in Europe after my service with BSC was terminated. In all of my work the support of M. R. Zigler and BSC was very helpful, and as an employee of CRALOG I tried to help whenever it was possible in encouraging Brethren programs. My wife continued to serve more directly in the distribution of welfare supplies in Bremen until we returned to America in 1951.

11. Brethren Service in Austria

by Ralph E. Smeltzer

I remember four phases in the development of Brethren Service in Austria: a good fast start, a long frustrating period without relief supplies, a time with supplies but insufficient staff, and finally a fruitful happy period with both supplies and staff.

BSC and the General Mission Board appointed me on November 14, 1945, to go to Japan to open Brethren relief work. For eight months I waited in vain for the necessary military clearance. So I asked M. R. ("Bob") Zigler to assign me elsewhere. He recommended that I try to get to Austria to establish a relief and rehabilitation program there. No investigation had been made, he said, as to whether it would be possible or what the procedure would be. Bob's style was to delegate responsibility to workers, put them on their own, and have confidence that they would do the job. That is what he did with me. He simply asked me to figure out how to get there, then to survey needs and submit program proposals to him.

On September 1, 1946, I entrained from Pomona, California, for Elgin, New Windsor, and Washington, leaving behind my wife, Mary, and daughters Janet (two) and Martha (six months). I visited the AFSC and MCC offices to find out how to get to Austria, then the President's Advisory Committee on Voluntary Foreign Aid, and the War Department's Civil Affairs Division. These latter offices sounded favorable and checked with General Mark Clark who happened to be visiting Washington that day from Vienna. General Clark was US High Commissioner in Austria and Commanding General of United States Forces in Austria (USFA). After he heard what we wanted to do, he said he would not only welcome the Brethren coming to Austria but would urge us to do so. He invited Bob and me to visit him immediately in Washington, but we said we felt this was unnecessary at the time. In Vienna later

Bob and I had a delightful informative conference with him.
The next day Bob and I visited Dr. L. von Kleinwächter,
envoy extraordinary and minister plenipotentiary of the
Austrian federal government in Washington. He greeted us
warmly, accepted our offer for relief and rehabilitation work in
his country, and immediately informed his government in Vienna. He visited our material aid and heifer projects at New
Windsor several days later and gave me letters of introduction
to Austria's chancellor, Leopold Figl, and several other officials.

I applied for my passport on September 20; General Clark
wired approval for my entry three days later; and the State
Department issued my passport and military permit on
September 30. Securing all this in ten days was almost un-
precedented at that time. I booked air passage to London on
October 5.

Bob suggested I first visit other Brethren projects in Europe in order to be better equipped for my Austrian assignment. On October 31 I received a wire from Bob saying he
desired to visit Austria within three weeks and would like for
me to have some program proposals ready for consideration by
then. So I hurried to Vienna on November 2.

Dr. Karl Heiser, chief, Public Health and Welfare Branch
of the US Allied Control Administration (USACA) and his
assistant, Anthony Podbielski, welcomed me and BSC to
Austria on behalf of the US occupation forces. They provided
all necessary military facilities and privileges including a billet
at the tiny *Goldener Hirsch* hotel, mess facilities, passes to
military installations, maps, post exchange facilities, and army
post office facilities.

Investigation soon indicated that the Reconstruction Committee of the Protestant Churches of Austria (RCPCA) needed
our assistance very much. It had received some relief supplies
from CWS and the Swiss Reconstruction Committee but had
no trucks to transport or distribute it. The motor of the 2½-ton
surplus army truck loaned to it by WCC was frozen and
broken. Austrian garages were not equipped to repair such
vehicles. American repair facilities were not available to
Austrians. So it was impossible to get the vehicle repaired. The
cost of shipping relief supplies throughout Austria by commer-
cial carrier was prohibitive, and trains were notoriously

vulnerable to pilferage. So one of the first things we did was to get WCC to put the vehicle in BSC's name in order that we could have it repaired at the Army Ordinance Center and serviced at the Army Exchange Service. We also requested WCC to provide us with a 2½-ton tractor/trailer from its Belgium-Holland-France operation, which it soon did.

In return for BSC's providing transportation and liaison with USACA, the RCPA agreed to: (1) store and handle Brethren Service supplies without cost to us at its service center, Hamburgerstrasse 3, Vienna V; and (2) provide us office space at its headquarters, Schellinggasse 12, Vienna I. Dr. Georg Traar was director of RCPCA and Hans Schager was manager of the service center. Since we were strangers to each other personally and ecclesiastically, and since we had the normal language difficulties, it took awhile for us to gain mutual trust and confidence, but it came and lasted in a magnificent manner. In time we also were able to provide helpful liaison between RCPCA and WCC/CWS. In a predominantly Roman Catholic country we helped the Protestant churches gain significant status and an enviable reputation for their relief and rehabilitation program.

Austria was divided into four occupation zones— American, Russian, French, and British. USACA facilities were available only in Vienna and the American zone. So I secured accreditation with UNRRA in order to receive travel permits for all zones and billeting, mess, and transportation facilities. Agricultural rehabilitation was another reason for linking up with UNRRA. As a result of conferences with Austrian UNRRA and American agriculture officials it was clear that Heifer Project should ship a quantity of heifers and bulls (for artificial breeding) to Austria through UNRRA facilities. Our agreement with UNRRA was signed November 21, 1946 with R. H. R. Parminter, Brigadier, chief of UNRRA mission to Austria.

Bob visited Austria from November 18—December 2, 1946. We made a six-day tour throughout the country to study conditions firsthand and to come to a decision on the validity of a half dozen projects I was recommending. Bob approved my project proposals, secured Eldon Burke's approval by telephone, arranged for the transfer of Helena Kruger, Grace Ritchey, and Roscoe Switzer to Austria, and cabled New

Windsor for a large quantity of food, bedding, shoes, soap, clothing, seeds, and livestock. Next we visited General Clark and the Austrian officials for whom I had letters of introduction. All gave hearty approval to our proposals.

Bob and I spent much time and energy during the next several months trying to work out an arrangement with WCC and CWS whereby these ecumenical agencies would serve as an umbrella under which denominational teams such as those of BSC in Austria, Germany, Poland, France, Holland, and Italy could operate, a plan in which such teams could maintain denominational identity within an overall ecumenical framework. We met with WCC and CWS leaders in Geneva and Bob met with CWS/WCC leaders in New York. At times we thought we would succeed but we kept finding resistance. Finally the proposed "ecumenical umbrella" plan fell through, and New Windsor agreed to send supplies and livestock directly to BSC, Austria.

Helena Kruger arrived on December 23, 1946. Our investigation soon disclosed that the *Volksdeutsche*—refugees of German ancestry from various eastern European countries— were the most needy, the most neglected, and the largest of all refugee or displaced-person groups in Austria. No relief agency would help them because of their ancestral relationship to ex-enemy Germany. The US Army and most agencies referred to the *Volksdeutsche* as "ex-enemy refugees." Neither the Army nor UNRRA recognized them as "eligible for assistance" though privately most Army officials admitted they were the best workers and the most appreciative, deserving, and desirable of the refugee groups.

Among those openly expressing this latter view was Col. McFeeley, USACA chief of the Displaced Persons Branch. On February 10, 1947, he approved a proposal for us to provide aid to *Volksdeutsche,* including helping them resettle in the US or other countries. Dr. Karl Heiser strongly opposed helping *Volksdeutsche* but because of his inferior rank McFeeley overrode his objections. Heiser left Austria a few months later, and Podbielski, his replacement, supported all our programs in every way. Helena Kruger and I also secured support and assistance for our refugee program from WCC's Ecumenical Refugee Commission, the Intergovernmental Committee for Refugees, and the RCPCA.

Our wisdom and persistence in helping the *Volksdeutsche* was widely recognized as time went on. One of the most complimentary remarks we ever received came from Captain Wright, our liaison with the US Army in Upper Austria. "In my judgment," he said, "BSC is the only true relief agency in Upper Austria. It gives to needy people without regard to race, creed, nationality, or past sins."

Roscoe and Grace Ritchey Switzer arrived February 2, 1947, with a truckload of school supplies, recreation equipment, toothbrushes, and other goods from Belgium. Roscoe immediately jumped into helping Hans Schager on warehousing and transportation. He drove and taught Austrians how to drive tractor-trailers throughout Austria delivering relief supplies. He was tops as a "scrounger-bargainer-buyer" of transport and relief supplies. Grace helped RCPCA with its *Ausspeisung* (feeding stations) for students and the aged, and provided food to Vienna's home economics school for its training program in cooking. She and Roscoe helped RCPCA set up a small clothing factory and shoe shop.

Our team got very frustrated because of not receiving any of the supplies or livestock that Bob, Eldon Burke, and I had ordered from New Windsor in December, 1946. While we kept writing, wiring, and pleading for these supplies, we started buying, bargaining, and securing other relief materials wherever we could get them: shoes from Czechoslovakia, food from the PX and CARE, blankets and shoes from the Army, six sewing machines, a half ton of cloth, shoe repair equipment, and leather from Belgium. Helena and Roscoe were most resourceful at this task.

This lack of supplies from the USA, however, began to endanger the continuation of our Austrian program. From the outside, Dr. Heiser of USACA hinted that we might have to leave Austria unless we could bring supplies as we had agreed. From the inside, BSC team morale hit a terrible low. Frustration, tensions, and feelings began to get out of control. Counseling staff members in this situation, trying to find constructive outlets, and developing satisfying alternative "side projects" was one of the most stressful periods I have had during my lifetime. Dissatisfaction caused Grace to return home in July. Three weeks later Roscoe became ill with yellow jaundice and spent four and one half months in military hospitals.

Soon after Helena Kruger's arrival, she and I visited the large Arsenal Refugee Camp in Vienna. We discovered ninety kindergarten children uncared for because their fathers were dead, were invalids, or in Russian prisons. Their mothers were cleaning bricks among the ruins of the bombed Vienna Arsenal in order to earn a little money. Among the mothers we found Frau Dulovitz and two other former schoolteachers who happily agreed to be employed as Brethren Service kindergarten teachers. In two or three months Helena had a model kindergárten in operation. She found a smoke-blackened room, secured windows somewhere, found paint for the walls, and got scrap lumber from the RCPCA warehouse. The refugees did the rest.

Her biggest hustling job, however, was the establishment of the Thalham refugee TB hospital in Upper Austria. *Volksdeutsche* refugees could not get into Austrian hospitals. Helena persuaded the government to make available an old Nazi labor camp of six run-down barracks at Thalham near St. Georgen. The Austrian government also agreed to pay the doctors and nurses and to supply the basic food ration. Three refugee doctors and several refugee nurses were available. From all kinds of sources Helena scrounged beds, bedside tables, mattresses, blankets, sheets, pillow cases, bed jackets, attendants' clothes, supplemental food, and gasoline for a hospital vehicle. Within two or three months the "hospital" opened in a primitive way with 125 patients. As soon as possible Helena supplied paint, fever thermometers, and wash basins. The Thalham staff always referred to her as "our angel."

On her own initiative, Helena asked her local church, Spring Creek, Hershey, Pennsylvania, to ship 1,440 hatching eggs and sixty-five sacks of feed to help rehabilitate Austria's poultry industry. The eggs arrived by air March 12, 1947—just in time for Easter. These eggs were the first material aid BSC in Austria received from the USA after its operations began in November, 1946, five months earlier. Since BSC-New Windsor helped the congregation send the eggs, we asked it to fly us 1,200 day-old chicks and to ship additional feed. The air-mailed chicks arrived via Pan American April 18 in good shape—to the great enjoyment of the flight crew, Austrian officials, and ourselves. Sixty-five sacks of feed arrived May 1.

We ordered and distributed similar shipments of chicks and feed in 1948 and 1949.

By late summer of 1947 significant quantities of material aid from New Windsor really began to arrive—a carload of cereal, a carload of dried fruits, 3,500 pairs of shoes, and other supplies—160,240 pounds by September 1. But then our staff was down to two, Helena and myself, so we worked night and day maintaining the program with RCPCA, distributing goods to *Volksdeutsche* refugees, and carrying out the projects to which we were committed in Upper Austria. Sometime before the Switzers left, we began pleading with Elgin for more workers, but none came. W. Harold Row and Wilbur Mullen visited us from December 2-11. After seeing our warehouses full and our shortage of help they stepped up BSC's effort to get us workers. They were favorably impressed with "Schager's storehouse" and our "teaming up with Traar." Their comment was, "This RCPCA center seems like New Windsor in reverse."

Helena returned to the USA on December 15, 1947. Fortunately Lois Rupel arrived a few weeks earlier to replace her. But I remember the tremendous workload I carried until Lois picked up full responsibilities in Upper Austria. In time she developed a fine material aid distribution system to refugee camps. She became "Miss Distribution Depot."

Our Vienna office administrative load became so heavy that we asked the Austrian employment bureau for a topflight secretary who could speak both English and German well. Among the candidates was Margit Hilsenrad who impressed us at once. She became our office anchor person—quiet, efficient, and perceptive. She served in this capacity until sometime after I left Austria. We never could have made it without her. Later she attended Manchester and Haverford Colleges and has now served with the World Health Organization in Geneva for several years.

To help provide more fresh milk for Vienna we worked out a plan with Mayor Körner, with Vienna's Association of Small Garden and Animals Keepers, and with our Heifer Project committee to purchase one hundred good milk goats in Switzerland, ship them by train to Vienna, and distribute them to needy families in Vienna's outskirts who had food and shelter for them in their "colony gardens." This project assignment fell to me in January, 1948. Mr. Dietrich of the Swiss government helped me buy and load them on the train at Gstaad, east of Lake Geneva. Then I rode in the freight car with the goats, tending them en route to Vienna. The International Red Cross helped on clearances and transportation. In Vienna the distribution was a gala occasion. Each recipient contracted to "pass on the first young to the Association of Small Garden and Animals Keepers to be distributed to another needy family under the same conditions."

Bob and I requested in December three hundred bred heifers, and six brown Swiss bulls to help rehabilitate Austria's dairy and artificial breeding program. In early 1948 we finally received eight scrawny purebred bulls of four dairy breeds. We were terribly embarrassed at their appearance and the Austrian officials bit their lips. But as time went on the sires developed into beautiful, fertile animals. When I revisited the modern Wels artificial breeding station in 1969, the managers remembered us, and proudly displayed photographs of the animals upon arrival, later as full-grown sires, and then some of their beautiful offspring. Next they took us to the barnyards to show us some of the bulls' handsome grandchildren and great-grandchildren now being used for artificial breeding.

Wonderful new workers arrived in early April, 1948 — Henry and Millie Long and Ira Gibbel. Henry and Millie became *Die helfenden Hände* (helping hands) to RCPCA in Vienna: maintaining their trucks, helping distribute monthly food packages to four hundred sick people, operating feeding kitchens and clothing distributions, developing the shoe repair shop, distributing five thousand Bibles and New Testaments to 250 pastors, and helping *Schwester* Dora Zimmermann maintain a kindergarten and day-care center for seventy-five children, and a study-play room for one hundred elementary-age children. Henry was so energetic and innovative it was hard to keep up with him. His photographic and publicity skills were most helpful in interpreting BSC's program in Austria and to the Brethren at home.

Refugee boys did not have vocational training opportunities due to lack of Austrian facilities and money. Ira developed a program with local Austrian schoolteachers in Linz to provide 150 boys the equivalent of a three-year vocational training course in one year of intensive night study. He did a great job turning out carpenters, mechanics, electricians, locksmiths, and automechanics. Also he developed a significant agricultural rehabilitation program. Six tons of seed potatoes, numerous varieties of hybrid seed corn, vegetables, and field seeds, and a garden tractor were given to federal agricultural stations in Upper Austria for experimental purposes. He supervised the distribution of many packages of garden seeds, and also the baby chicks.

Twenty-one months after leaving my family in Pomona I was able to secure military clearance for them to join me in Vienna. It was difficult to secure clearance because of the shortage of housing; they were the first civilian relief agency family permitted to come. They arrived on May 5, 1948, at Tulln Airport. Imagine my feelings when the children walked past me at the gate ahead of their mother and neither they nor I recognized each other. As two and three-and-a-half-year-old children it took some time for them to learn to know me as their father.

When Lois Rupel left in November, 1948, Rosemary Block, a nurse, replaced her. Not only did she continue the relief distributions to refugees, but she organized additional health projects and helped up-grade Thalham Hospital. She and Ira were quite a team in Upper Austria. What one could not think of the other could. Always busy, always on the go, Rosemary just kept rolling along.

Sometime before the Longs' return to the USA in April, 1949, Denny Garber came to learn their jobs and become our representative to RCPCA. He not only found a job at the center, but a wife, Friedl. He became one of our permanent contributions to Austria, staying to become a professional computer operator and Vienna homeowner.

For thirty-two months Austria was my home and Austrian Brethren Service my life. When I left with my family on June 23, 1949, it was with a feeling of solid accomplishment, inspired by Bob Zigler's great spirit of confidence in us and sustained by a dedicated group of faithful team members. Those who carried on and came later will have to complete the story of BSC in Austria. The Austrian government gave me a medallion for my services. Its inscription read, "Das Wiener Kind dankt seinen Helfern" (The Viennese child thanks you for your help).

12. Brethren Service in Poland

by Opal D. Stech

The impetus for the starting of home economics at the Central Agricultural College (SGGW) came from the many professors already on the staff who had received their doctorates from Cornell University, New York. While living in the United States they had observed the contribution that home economics had made to home, family, and community life. It was their feeling that home economics could do the same for their home country, Poland. I concurred with their idea after working in Poland.

In Poland any project must be supported and approved by the government. When government bureaucracy is involved anywhere the tempo of progress is often slow. The government in Poland was cooperative, recognizing that what we were attempting to accomplish was greatly needed in their country. It was true, after December 15, 1948, the scope of our work was altered due to their request. We were pleased to have approximately ninety students enrolled during the second year.

When I visited Poland in the summer of 1966, seventeen years after our work, many of the ninety students gathered for a reunion with us. It was gratifying to hear of their pride in what they had been able to do to increase efficiency in their homes and to improve community life.

When we went to Warsaw in 1947 we estimated that approximately ninety percent of the city was in ruins due to the destruction of World War II. Sanitation was a real problem, so it was not surprising that the first person we requested to be

---

Editor's note. Brethren Service work in Poland began in 1945 with the first shipment of livestock by the Heifer Project and continued until 1949 when the Polish government asked foreign agencies to leave. Early work centered on community rehabilitation at Ostroda, but after 1947 increasing emphasis was placed on the exchange of students and faculty between the USA and Poland. Areas of concentration were agriculture and home economics. Opal Stech here describes her experience as a teacher in Warsaw.

added to our staff was a Ph.D. in bacteriology. Tuberculosis was on the increase especially among young people. The scientific understanding from our teaching was readily accepted. Polish people were among early contributors to the scientific field, so they were ready for such an approach. Home conditions were not ideal for sanitation. However, we could show by means of a culture plate the difference in the number of bacteria from a hot-water-rinsed dish and from dishes only being cleaned of foreign particles in cold water.

Collaboration with other agencies not only increased total contributions but allowed us as workers some observations that were very challenging. My zest for the field of nutrition was greatly influenced by what I observed in the *Don Suisse* camp. Their objective was to take young children who were malnourished as campers for a period of from four to six weeks. By so doing, they hoped to prevent tuberculosis and to effect permanently full development of the human potential. I recall visiting one group of young children arriving at the camp. They could hardly carry their small suitcases of clothing. At their first meal they sat almost silent, yet were easily irritated, and they ate meagerly. The observers knew at the same time they were actually hungry.

I revisited the camp and these same children in less than a month. The dining room was noisy at mealtime, and the quantity of food being consumed was alarming. Games and fun were being enjoyed by most campers. I have often stated I can tell in myself how differently I feel when I have been on a poor diet for four days. Incidents such as these we saw convince nutritionists that food, the right amount and kind, is basic in the development of persons, communities, and nations. Thus food is essential for international order.

We felt there were many brilliant people in Poland. Yet without the exchange of ideas and contact of technological progress many individuals were living in primitive conditions. We were fortunate in having the opportunity to take some modern equipment with us. Most individuals who have traveled in Europe have seen laundry items washed in lakes and streams. Not only does this make for a difficult task but it lacks sanitation. We took an electric washing machine to Poland. In our department at times we had to guard against the curious mechanic wanting to tear it apart to see how it was constructed. Polish individuals in a demonstration audience would often take off one of their garments and throw it into the washer. They were eager to determine if the machine would clean any garment that was not American made.

The kitchen unit we took from Nappanee, Indiana, was used to demonstrate new ideas. Polish carpenters did a beautiful job of making, from wood, units for our foods laboratory. I spent many hours attempting to teach the use of UNRRA equipment I found on the shelves of the vocational schools. This had been sent into Poland without instructors, and in some cases Polish personnel could not even identify it.

The eagerness of the Polish people to be of service to their fellow citizens was very impressive. At the request of some American friends I visited a hospital near Ostroda to determine their most urgent need for equipment. I was amazed at the effort that had been made by doctors to salvage parts from various hospitals, then reassemble them as useful equipment for operations and medical care. Later when I delivered the gift of obstetrical equipment, tears came to the eyes of the doctors as they fondly handled each piece they unpacked from the boxes.

In Warsaw we were able to locate only one person with dietetic training. Many years before she had received some training in Iowa. The government requested that I spend more time teaching in the field of institutional management. The government had spent time and money in developing community housing, but there are few trained personnel in these projects. In this living arrangement all individuals left their living quarters for the day. Women as well as men were employed. During pregnancy, a woman's leave began after six months and lasted until the baby was six weeks old. The small baby then went along to a factory nursery.

The housing units provided child nurseries, cooperative laundries, and institutional group feeding. Children from three to eighteen years were under the control of the ministry of education. In 1966 one of my questions as I returned to Poland, was: "Do families still live in cooperative housing arrangements?" The answer I received was "No. People need a family structure." This was another example of the willingness to experiment but also of their wisdom in changing when they found they still had problems.

Brethren Service in Poland

It seems the Polish people have always had a life of struggle. They endure hardships and tackle problems with an eagerness I have never seen equalled. Their sense of humor has brought them through many a crisis. What college or university student in America would sleep on a wooden-slat, triple-deck, no-mattress bed, wrap himself in wool blankets to study, and attempt to live mainly on a potato diet? We lived on the top floor of a house which had been converted into a dormitory. Our usual welcome at noon was to have the steps of the top flight of stairs filled with seated individuals awaiting our assistance.

Craftsmanship and quality of work continued to command pride while we were working in Poland. I recall, as we were planning and building the first cafeteria at the Central Agricultural College, how the craftsmen who had developed the steam-jacketed kettles insisted they must be placed in the center of the floor plan. They wanted the kettles to be the first thing a person would see on entering the kitchen. Efficiency and energy-saving within a job were not of prime consideration.

In Poland I became aware of a desire for the full development of professional people. Women as well as men were encouraged to reach their maximum human potential.

13. The Kaltenstein Project

by Byron P. Royer

During 1948 and 1949 BSC played a crucial role in the conversion of the 115-room Kaltenstein Castle in Southeastern Germany from a Nazi detention center to a "village" for refugee youth. The seventy tons of food and clothing, contributed in that first year, became the primary factor in the decision as to whether or not this model German "Boys' Town" would be organized.

Pastor Arnold Dannenmann, of the German YMCA, had become painfully aware of the fact that approximately 100,000 youth were roaming around the country, homeless, and often supporting themselves with black-market activities. He had learned through the YMCA prison work that many youth were in prison only because they had neither identification papers nor a home to go to. The postwar government was warm toward Pastor Dannenmann's request for the use of Kaltenstein Castle as a home for these youth, but a most important ingredient was missing—food and clothing for a whole youth village of one hundred boys.

Dwight Horner, who was a member of the Church of the Brethren, a former YMCA worker with war prisoners and, by then, a US State Department staff member, had the answer. He proposed that BSC provide the food and clothing and, further, that they send a Brethren Service person to be loaned to the German YMCA as a social work consultant. As a result, I was assigned to this project and, with my family, lived for a year in the castle itself, working directly with the German staff to implement Dannenmann's dream. This and the dedicated work of Dr. and Mrs. Eldon Burke in Bremen were the earliest efforts in refugee relief in Germany following World War II.

Kaltenstein can be seen from any direction you approach it. It is located on the top of a hill, looking down over the small county seat, Vaihingen-Enz. The walls of the original building, earlier protected by a moat, are ten feet thick solid masonry, a formidable fortress against attack in its day.

The present castle has been expanded to 115 rooms and now boasts a central heating unit. It was more comfortable in the wintertime with the central heating in operation than in the summer when the stone walls never seem to warm up completely. The outer buildings, built later, were well suited for a variety of shops for training the boys in a trade—cooking, baking, shoe repair, metal-working, woodworking, farming. Masters in each of these trades served as the teachers.

Very early, the staff and I developed a system of "Kaltenstein money," which was earned according to guidelines first formulated by the staff. Later the boys had a voice in determining this kind of community policy. A small percentage of the money could be converted into German marks, making possible small purchases in the town. Most of the Kaltenstein money was used to "buy" Brethren Service clothing. As a result of this plan, the boys soon learned how to be financially responsible—in contrast to their black-market past.

The most difficult venture during the first year centered in the all-out effort to encourage these former Nazi youth to govern themselves. This seemed totally beyond their comprehension at first, even though we of the staff were dedicated to self-government as a principle. We reassured the youth time after time that we were in earnest about turning responsibility over to them.

On the day of the "big fire," the leaders were finally convinced that the year's work was worth doing. Across a small valley, a fire broke out in the wooden barracks that housed a number of *Volksdeutsche* (refugees of German origin who had come from behind the Iron Curtain). The youth rushed over and, at some physical risk, helped carry out the refugees' only possessions before the barracks burned down. Some of the local villagers stood by without helping, apparently relieved to see this eye-sore to their community eliminated.

As the boys returned to the castle after the fire, they called a special parliament meeting and, without any adult help, voted to share what they had with the *Volksdeutsche*. They decided that each boy would contribute a two-weeks' allowance in Kaltenstein money and that this would be spent for clothing and blankets for those who were burned out.

They acted very sensitively at two points. First, they exempted any boy who had recently arrived and was still in dire need. Second, they appointed what the Brethren would call a "deacons' committee," to visit the refugees and survey the need. They invited me to be a part of this committee and to join them in this visit. Needless to say, this voluntary action of former Nazi youth brought tears to the eyes of more than one leader.

The second high point of the first year came during the Advent season—as Christmas approached. The youth joined all Germany in celebrating the Sundays of Advent. The head of the American High Commission in Germany, John J. McCloy, attended one of these Advent dinners. Mrs. McCloy, speaking fluent German, was the "hit" of the day with the boys.

As Christmas approached, a deacon, the wife of the Kaltenstein manager, and Ruth Royer spent long hours preparing personalized gifts for the nearly one hundred youth. This was done with loving care after making every effort to learn what would bring each boy the greatest joy in the holiday season. The youth dressed up in their very attractive BSC clothing for the opening of gifts. Their faces lit up when they saw even the most simple gifts and, later, their lusty singing became their "thank you's."

Not only is *Jugenddorf* (youth village) Schloss Kaltenstein continuing at the present time (1974) but there are also approximately fifty additional projects which have been spawned by this agency of the German YMCA. I have remained in touch with my former colleagues, visiting them in person in 1970. In 1974, Ruth and I were invited to return as the guests of the German YMCA and, as of the time of this writing, were hoping to accept this invitation in 1975.

The work at Kaltenstein modeled a very important principle of early Brethren Service work—the principle calling for the staff to remain flexible enough to move into areas of great need, helping local personnel to take on responsibility for their own programs, and then leaving the program with the local staff in order to turn to areas of greater need. This principle represented one of the greatest strengths of the early BSC program. As soon as the need at Kaltenstein was met, the program was left in other capable hands.

14. Interchurch Service to Greek Villages

by M. R. Zigler

In **1950** I was challenged by two officials of the Church of England to consider serving in Greece in order to help reestablish the farmers on the land in the northern part of the country. Already at this time BSC administration in the US was considering how to retreat from Europe, hoping that the needs had been met as far as outside help was essential.

Investigation revealed that about two million Greek farmers had been driven from their farms as a result of the civil war that followed liberation. And this came after four hundred years of Turkish occupation and after the Second World War in which the Germans and Italians made war in Greece. It was also discovered that there were about two million farmers located in refugee camps who should be returned to their home villages in northern Greece. The Greek government took a census of homeless people and classified them according to the villages from which they had come. These families were delivered by military trucks back to their devastated homes. They found their houses without windows, floors, or roofs. Every wooden item had been used by the occupying forces for firewood, cooking, or heating purposes. Farms had grown up in weeds and brush. Animals had been slaughtered.

The refugees were provided with requisition papers from the government which allowed each head of a family materials for one door and one window, and seeds and fertilizer for one acre of ground. For the most part, these materials were never made available. It was soon understood that the farmers would need large quantities of seeds, simple farm tools, clothing and food, and practically everything required for sustaining family life.

Here, as everywhere else in Europe, the Brethren had no beachhead on which to land and begin operations. A letter of introduction from WCC at Geneva was presented to the Archbishop of Athens and All Greece, Bishop Spyridon. Fortunately, in 1945, Brethren Service, through the Heifer Project, had delivered six bulls to establish an artificial insemination program near Athens. Such programs had been successful in other areas. When the archbishop discovered that BSC was responsible for this program and gave promise of a wider range of activities in agriculture for the refugee farmers in northern Greece, he began proposing other suggestions that might be helpful to the people of his country.

He finally suggested that he would contact the department of agriculture of the Greek government and seek cooperation in developing a plan and furnishing possible resources. A letter of invitation was sent to Geneva along with an invitation by the government, which opened the way for services for refugees by the churches and through the Greek Orthodox church. In view of the fact that the Brethren resources came entirely from the United States, the US government officials in Greece were approached on the matter. When they gave encouragement, the Brethren Service home office was informed of the need for further resources. It was necessary to set aside funds and grant authorization for sending persons into the area of Epirus at Ioannina along the Albanian border. In due time clearances were made. Soon Edson Sower and Dean Neher were on their way traveling in jeeps from Germany and Austria through Yugoslavia to Greece to begin operations.

It was soon evident that the resources of the Church of the Brethren would not be sufficient to provide for the needs of the people. Therefore, other denominational agencies represented in WCC were urged to join in the cooperative enterprise. The first approach was made to the Lutheran World Federation through Dr. S. C. Michelfelder, its executive secretary at Geneva. This need was presented to Dr. Franklin Fry, chairman of LWF, on one of his visits to Geneva. Dr. Fry and Dr. Michelfelder presented the opportunity to the meeting of the Federation in Washington. Dr. Fry responded by letter as follows: "The Lutheran World Federation at its meeting today approved $5,000 and the appointment of a man for the Greek team, without a murmur. Yours for peace. Franklin Fry."

The Disciples of Christ, under the leadership of Robert Tobias, decided to participate. They placed a man on the team and provided resources. The Presbyterian Church, USA, under the leadership of Charles Arbuthnot, appropriated funds. The

Interchurch Service to Greek Villages

Evangelical United Brethren, the American Baptist Convention, and the Swedish Lutheran Church joined in the movement. The Episcopalians expressed interest via Bishop Larned through special gifts. Later the Evangelical and Reformed group and the Methodist Commission for Relief and CWS began to associate with the movement. The Mennonites joined by placing two men on the team and helping through material aid.

As the idea grew and the experiment began to prove satisfactory, the British Council of Churches, the Danish Council of Churches, and the Council of Churches of Holland joined in the support. CWS provided funds for special items in the program. The cooperation of men in the field with varied backgrounds developed an unusual pattern of operation, both in the creation of policy and the establishment of a field staff that was difficult to name. This movement finally was named "Inter-Church Service to Greek Villages."

The movement represented action by a group of churches for which WCC could not be responsible. But in accordance with the charter of the World Council, assistance was given by providing a liaison representative from the staff of the Inter-Church Aid and Service to Refugees Committee. The facilities of the treasurer were made available.

The supporting agencies held their meetings in Geneva, Switzerland, and reported to the Inter-Church Aid and Service to Refugees Committee regularly. The informational services of the World Council participated fully in giving information to the religious and secular press and by creating materials describing the objectives of the program and of activities carried on in Greece.

The archbishop was certain that the most needy area was around Ioannina, a city with a population of forty thousand. The city had many small shops and offered handmade merchandise. There was telephone and telegraph service. There were no railroads in the area and bus travel was strenuous and tiresome. The only plane service was from Athens.

The farmers lived in villages near water supplies. Each village was supposed to have a priest, a schoolteacher, and a government official. These three persons formed a committee to which our workers were assigned to develop agricultural programs in the community. We did not need a large overhead in Athens or in Ioannina, but there had to be someone at each place to expedite the shipping of materials and the transfer of workers. Therefore, a team house had to be found and rented. This was not easy. With the help of the Greek people of Ioannina, adequate housing was provided so that each team member would have a place to keep his personal belongings.

It was clear from the beginning that a person working in a village could not stay there continuously and have good health. The policy was established that each worker would go to the village on Monday and return on Saturday to headquarters to spend the weekend for reporting, consulting, and resting. Each team member selected an interpreter to be with him. Generally there was only one team member to a village.

Representatives coming back from the villages soon were able to anticipate the needs. It appeared that the first thing to do was to divide seeds for the gardens and the fields, and then food and clothing. For some reason the Greek people had lost the art of preserving food. Therefore, a call was made for glass jars for canning food. Millions of jars were brought in through the relief agencies and used by the villagers to preserve fruits and vegetables for winter use. In fact, all sorts of things were needed, including sewing machines and ploughs. There had to be training classes to teach people how to use the available gifts.

Heifer Project was able to furnish cows to some farmers and institutions that could provide the animals with food. The difficulty in offering heifers to farmers was that the animal could be given only to a person who had feed enough for the cow. This really meant that the person who received the gift had some resources above the average Greek farmer.

Probably the most thrilling part of the program was the arrival of little chicks, or eggs. However, it was one of the most difficult items to handle. In utilizing the 4-H Club method, little chicks were given to farmers through young people who learned to raise chickens and market them. Both heifer and chicken projects demanded that those receiving the gifts should share as quickly as possible with near neighbors. As people began to have poultry, milk, and butter to sell, they could then buy shoes and clothing for their families.

In 1953 the archbishop wrote: "I send you my warmest thanks and congratulations for the work that has been done in missionary faith.... I will be glad indeed to meet the director and I hope that in the coming summer one or two young Greek men, students of theology, will be added to the team working in Epirus.... I take this chance to express the feeling of gratitude and the love of the villagers who were helped by the team of young men that may God always bless."

The first members of the Greek team, Edson Sower and Dean Neher, heard a story that sounded like a myth. A long tunnel had been closed for one hundred years which, if it could be opened, would enable a large area of land to be reclaimed. One day some team workers were climbing over a small mountain. It was located about thirty miles from Ioannina with only a road for donkey travel and pedestrians. With difficulty a jeep might get through. Looking down to the valley below, they saw a series of green spots, forty or more feet apart. They decided to investigate and dug under a green spot. They discovered a tunnel that was about a mile long. At some places the tunnel was fifty feet under ground and at other places less deep. It had been built during the Turkish invasion to drain the valley.

The name of the valley in which the tunnel was discovered was Pontikates-Delo. The only equipment available for the digging were buckets and ropes. It took much faith to start on this project. Many days of work were required before the Greek people had confidence that there was a tunnel and that it could be reclaimed to drain the land. The foreign team continued to work. It was dangerous work because, as they would remove the debris, often the sides would cave in. One time one of the men was caught by a falling rock, but fortunately he was able to escape with a minor back injury.

It was really a dirty job and one of slow progress. Finally, a priest came one day to observe the work of the team. He removed his robe and went down into the tunnel to help dig the dirt and fill the buckets. After that, willing villagers went down into the tunnel each day and worked long and hard, digging out mud and water which they lifted to the surface bucketful by bucketful. One member of the team described the organization as follows: "The past week I worked in the tunnel every day; there are usually six or seven of us below the ground.... Cave-ins have troubled us a great deal.... I find work in the hole rather exciting in spite of all the mud and water, the small size of the tunnel, which necessitates cramped legs and back, the bad air (matches will not burn there), the black smoke from the acetylene torches and dim lights.... At the present time there are twelve men working on the project, hours seven to twelve and three to six. We are providing the workers with a good noon meal."

The time schedule for the project stretched out. The job was estimated to take a year and a half. It actually took three years for the men from America, Britain, Sweden, and Holland, with the help of the Greek people to finish it. The Greek Orthodox church authorized a very important dedication ceremony on November 16, 1953.

When the tunnel was completed and the water drained, two hundred acres of fertile soil were available to the people of three small villages. A number of years after the opening of the tunnel we heard reports that the tunnel had closed again, that the land was becoming a swamp. Then a representative reported in Ioannina that the tunnel was still open, that the land was being farmed, that they had found water ten feet below the ground near the good land, and that the villagers were coming down from the lowlands to the villages where people had lived for several centuries. The completion of the tunnel gave a sense of victory. At the same time reports went to all the agencies supporting it, and through these agency headquarters to the supporters. A cable was received at Geneva with only two words, "Tunnel completed."

Now there seemed to be freedom to move in a larger way in the whole area around Ioannina. Immediately a program was launched to include:

1. Improvement in agriculture, in planning methods, seeds, use of vital land, use of tractors and equipment, rebuilding soil by crop rotation and fertilizer, new crops, and experiments in growing feeds for special projects, for cows and poultry.

2. Gardening and home economics, introduction of new seeds, canning methods and proper cooking, dietetics.

3. Extension of orchards, tree planting, bee culture.

4. Social work, holding village conferences to develop community cooperation, 4-H Clubs, clubs for home improvement.

5. Continuation of special projects with bees, chickens, dairy cattle, hybrid corn, garden seeds, and introduction of other machinery.

Interchurch Service to Greek Villages

As is usual in relief and rehabilitation projects, team members changed frequently, and in a short time a whole new staff was at work. The director of the unit that followed the first group, Orville Sherman, said in his annual report: "I am pleased with the team's efforts, the interest and enthusiasm of its members. Due to the increase of qualified personnel we are accomplishing more and morale is at a good level. Relations with public officials are good, the Greek army being most sympathetic, which is important in this border area; and the Greek church has expressed its deep thanks and continues to render all possible assistance. The team program is carried out in each village."

There were many difficulties to face in Greece, and especially in Epirus. This field location was along the Albanian border and in a military zone, which, by the nature of the situation, demanded more than usual clearance for operation and reportings to the church, the civil government, and the military. Furthermore, perhaps the most difficult thing to achieve was trust on the part of the local people, where distribution of food, clothing, seeds, heifers, poultry, and other items had to be transferred from the givers abroad through young inexperienced foreigners. The presence of a team of youth workers was hard to explain. Why did they come without special preparation and skills, and for what purpose? What was their motive? What prompted this expression of love in the interest of peace and goodwill?

The first encounter in each local village was with the head of the civil government, the schoolteacher, and the priest. These three had to assume the responsibility to open doors to the strangers. It was difficult to explain how Protestantism could work together for the common good on behalf of the Greek people, without discrimination, through the sponsorship of the Orthodox church. The greatest fear seemed to rest in the possibility that these Protestant representatives might proselyte the members of the Orthodox faith.

Although the team members were young, simply prepared for an encounter with hungry and homeless people, with no Greek language background, with limited resources at hand to share, coming from several denominations and nations, facing the needs of the villages being rebuilt by the refugee farmers, they came through the experience with confidence in their cause. Material monuments have not been erected to register the presence of these peacemakers. But in the countryside of Greece there are markers in the hearts of the villagers and farmers. There is and will be for a long time evidence of the results of artificial insemination and the heifer project. The saving of seeds from one season to the next continues in a process of sharing. Stability for family life on the farms was made possible by helping farmers to have enough feed to maintain healthy growing flocks and herds. It took many years to develop a breed of chickens of a new and large type that could withstand disease and climate of the area. In anything attempted there was discouragement and hopelessness for a time.

It is likely that the holding force in keeping the staff members at this task of rehabilitation was spiritual. One of the government officials at Ioannina said, "Although we value and appreciate highly the material help you have brought to the church, the school, and the farmers, the greatest contribution has been the spirit in which the young people have served." At length he said, "We have been thrust in a needy situation, as a nation; your help has given us hope and faith. And above all, you have come in person to help us in every way possible to rebuild our home and community life. You have also given us a new faith in our church."

15. The Refugee Resettlement Program

by Joseph B. Mow

First impressions are often the most memorable. Such was the first day I was in Vienna in June, 1949 when Ralph Smeltzer showed me around for my job in refugee resettlement. It was his last day as director of BSC in Austria. The night before he had asked me to read through a foot-high pile of files, which I did in a hotel in the Soviet sector of Vienna. After falling to sleep at about one a.m., already exhausted before arriving, I was awakened at two a.m. by two Soviet army officers wanting to see my passport and other documents. I was sure I would be the first Brethren refugee sent to a Siberian work camp. But they left me there, not without further suspicion I am sure, and the next night we did find a room in the international sector. But I went on becoming acquainted with all the officials I would have to deal with that day, along with helping Ralph buy leather goods and other parting souvenirs.

During these early months we were trying to interview *Volksdeutsche* refugees for resettlement in the USA. Each of them had to have an individual affidavit of support from an American citizen, which affidavit had to show all the assets of the American sponsor. Rather complete interviews were necessary to make the qualifications and life story of the refugees appealing to potential sponsors. It was a difficult and slow method of resettlement. The one refugee I most remember is the harried man who had come over from Hungary the night before and appeared in our office on Schellinggasse in Vienna. He had immediate needs for food and shelter which we ourselves could not quite provide, but I interviewed him thoroughly for resettlement, saying we could only wait for somebody to become interested. At the very end I had a vague recollection about some date-lines in the law. So I read the law and found that this man was not permitted to come as a refugee because he had escaped too late from behind the Iron Curtain. It was both the documentation and some of these arbitrary provisions which made refugee resettlement rather heartrending. We did document over twenty-five families, many of whom were sponsored by Brethren in the USA.

Instead of the individually oriented *Volksdeutsche* program, BSC joined in the CWS "blanket assurance" program for persons not of German origin who had been forced laborers in Germany. The Brethren provided 1,250 sponsors, in effect sight unseen, for whom we were to select displaced persons (DP's) in Austria and Germany. So in October, 1949, we went on a hurried program of selection, from among DP's registered through the International Refugee Organization (IRO) and CWS. Most of them were Ukrainian and Orthodox, as our assurance was for farm help. As it happened, the US Displaced Persons Act had a quota of farmers, such that other DP's could only get visas if a high percentage went as farmers. The Brethren blanket assurance therefore broke a large logjam in the "pipeline" of DP applicants for all the churches.

My first encounter with such selection was in the British Zone of southern Austria. It is well to remember that there had been a repatriation program of DP's back to behind the Iron Curtain shortly before, and that almost no resettlement program had grown beyond a few token placements in all the rest of the world. My interpreter and I interviewed some forty families a day for a week in well-organized interviews by IRO. For each family I was in the unfortunate position of having to play God, for they thought that if I turned them down they would be repatriated. Only shortly before some had been killed in forced repatriation. In any case, their having been well screened, I gave assurances to about two thirds of those I saw, and they were overjoyed. Later I found out that one of the women I had rejected, upon investigation on a different assurance, was found to have murdered thirteen men.

This selection process went on at a furious pace for over two months, sometimes involving interviewing sixty families per day. We went to Linz, Salzburg, Innsbruck, and Bregenz in Austria, and Munich, Ulm, and Augsburg in Bavaria. Byron Royer did some interviewing near Stuttgart, and Kurtis Naylor near Kassel. By mid-December we had selected all 1,250 displaced persons, and were warning New Windsor of a coming flood of refugees.

It took about three months for each DP to secure a visa

and start to travel through Bremerhaven for New Windsor. Our interview notes were sent in the meantime, but we did not have time to do complete ones, assuming that a more careful interview could be done by Ruth Early in New Windsor. By March, 1950, she was inundated with people, interviews, and placement arrangements as the DP's arrived in masses. At our end we had completed our interviewing program before many churches had even started. Fortuitously, this meant that we had the best selection of persons to choose from, even though a variety of natural complaints came back to us. Thereafter we had only to replace a few selections when they were turned down for any of a hundred reasons by the Displaced Persons Commission, the State Department, or the Immigration and Naturalization Service.

The situation in the selection for all churches was so crucial that CWS asked me to take over the office in Schweinfurt in Germany, the conduct of Brethren selection having been quite astounding to all others. So Don Durnbaugh, Margit Hilsenrad, and I spent from January to April selecting refugees and operating the office in Schweinfurt, while continuing our interviewing of individual *Volksdeutsche* and other activities. When the CWS offices were officially changed to operation under WCC, I was officially seconded to WCC, and became head of DP resettlement to the USA, first for the British Zone of Germany in Hamburg, and then in the Munich area. Conducting large offices with the many intricate details of processing applications was a very massive job, so my recollections are of immense amounts of work and the daily agony of presiding over the fate of hundreds of people.

There was one interlude, in the spring of 1950, of planning the first Brethren Peace Seminar in Vienna, which, as it turned out, Earl Garver and Don Durnbaugh actually conducted while I was in Hamburg. The seminar was part work camp in a student hostel in Vienna, and had outside speakers each week. BSC kept me on their fraternal list, even though I was employed elsewhere, and thus I was able to attend the BSC annual conferences, and two of the peace conferences, in England and in Holland, and go to meetings in Kassel, Stuttgart, and Vienna on occasion, as well as to several work camps.

The deadline for giving assurances to DP's was July 31, 1951. Two days before, the US decided to admit a group of

Mongols on the ground that, having been in Europe for seven centuries, they were a white race. In those two days we submitted the names of all these Kalmuks, and I took the completed list to the head of the Munich DP Commission at 11:50 p.m. We then had to interview all of them, paying particular attention to the group placement aspects of this group of Buddhists who had lived in the Don region and Astrakhan region of Russia. Thus we came to know rather intimately their religion and culture and history. The Brethren decided to sponsor their resettlement in November, 1951.

In January I returned to the US to join Don Durnbaugh, Mary Coppock, Ben Bushong, the staff at New Windsor, and many others in arranging their placement. Don and Mary made arrangements for about a hundred of them to settle in New Mexico, but these Kalmuks became lonely and decided to return to the East. When the Kalmuks did arrive they overflowed New Windsor, so we also operated out of the migrant labor camp run by Seabrook Farms in southern New Jersey. We secured jobs for all the men in Philadelphia and in northern New Jersey, who then arranged housing and brought the rest of their families. By the end of March we had placed them all, which was a rather exhausting feat. A typical day involved leaving New Windsor with a car full at six a.m., going to the employment office, and then translating for each of them as they got their jobs. Then we had to care for their temporary housing, and a hundred other errands with respect to their finances, health, and adjustment.

Overall I am sure that the refugee resettlement project was a very worthwhile one. Without the churches almost nothing would have been done to solve this postwar problem. Most of the DP's secured other jobs after their first ones, but the effort of many church sponsors was a demonstration of their concern and a test of their understanding of other people. It was a very large, tangible, and difficult area of work; the Brethren contribution was recognized as far out of proportion to the size of the church and brought considerable recognition to the Brethren Service program.

16. The High School Exchange Program

by John H. Eberly

At **the time** Brethren Service took the first steps to enter the student exchange program in a significant way, and for which it later received considerable recognition, many exchange programs were big business. But up to this time, these programs had pretty much if not entirely avoided any responsibility for teenagers. Exchanges were in the categories of specialists in a variety of fields, and primarily involved advanced academic students. In fact, the exchange program professionals passed off such things as home and family hospitality and a high school experience for teenagers as ridiculous if not impossible.

It was in this field in 1949 that Brethren Service initiated the first high school exchange program with the help of the United States military occupation authorities in Germany and with Germans themselves. BSC brought to America ninety German teenagers, sixteen to eighteen years old, each to live a year with a family and to attend the local high school. How did this come about?

In Paris (1949), a conference was in session discussing how to accelerate food production, especially in Germany. M. R. Zigler is reported to have told the UNESCO group about the agricultural exchange of ten young Polish farm youth who were brought to the United States by BSC in 1947 to live with farm families. It was hoped that they would learn some farming methods which they could take back and use to improve food production in their country. The idea was picked up by a member of the Rural Education section of the Food and Agriculture Agency (FAO) of the United Nations stationed in Frankfurt, Germany. BSC had been active in Germany for some time in relief work with war prisoners, refugees, and with work camps. Heifer Project had been permitted to bring the first animals to Germany in May, 1949, for then it was decided that "food grains" could be spared to increase "fodder grains" for animals. It was in this setting of need, especially to help German refugees whose homes had been destroyed by the bombings and whose means of livelihood was so limited, that BSC started conversations with FAO on something to help them. It could not be resettlement; it could not involve youth of the age of the young Polish farmers because these youth were out on their own. The refugee camps did have sixteen to eighteen-year-olds.

The first thought on the part of BSC centered largely on food but they also considered the betterment of relationships between Germany and the USA. Brethren had unusual interest in Germany because of their historical origin in that country and because a large percentage of Brethren were of German descent. So next to food, or perhaps underlying all other reasons, was that which was believed and hoped to be a Brethren mission in the world—that of peace.

The concept of student exchange was not unfamiliar to Brethren because of the Polish experiment of 1947, which ten years later was taken up again and became a major agricultural project with BSC. And this writer, while serving in Italy in the latter half of 1948, representing Heifer Project, had proposed a scheme to UNRRA/CASAS, the coordinating relief agency for that country, to bring fifteen Italian youth of 4-H age to America to be guests of the 4-H clubs for the purpose of transplanting this idea to that country. This exchange did not get far because questions of religious proselytizing were raised, though BSC had been quite well accepted in relief activities in Italy for several years. The BSC work in Italy was closed out in early 1949, and some personnel moved to Frankfurt in February.

About the middle of July, 1949, the possibility of a program was given the Heifer Project office in Frankfurt for development. Already it was fairly clear that BSC was interested in sixteen- to eighteen-year-olds in the refugee camps visiting for a year in Brethren homes in the United States and attending the local high school of the host family. Heifers were already being distributed to those refugee families able to support them. Selection of these recipient families was made by a German committee, one member of which was the director of German refugee affairs. With his help it was proposed to find selected teenagers in the refugee camps for the exchange. FAO would finance the travel and BSC would assume responsibility with the host family, the local school, and church for the year's stay in the United States. The number for this first trial group was set at fifty, both boys and girls.

Now came a new problem. It was soon apparent that this project would entail a great deal more than what either BSC or FAO was accustomed to have facilitated through CRALOG. This was not an overseas shipment of cargo. Here was a proposal to send fifty youth, children in the German sense, not a shipment of relief goods. In addition to the unprecedented responsibility (because they were considered children by their parents) to be assumed by the sponsoring agencies, there was the logistics of passports, visas, as well as many personal matters having to do with safety and well-being. BSC could not clear all this with FAO, so a third partner was enlisted. This was the Cultural Affairs Department of the High Commissioner for the Occupation of Germany (HICOG).

Now there were three partners in the project—BSC, FAO, and HICOG itself. Negotiations which began with FAO were gradually and completely shifted to the Cultural Affairs people at Bad Nauheim, Germany, though FAO continued its interest in the rural youth selected for the exchange and put some money in the program for a time.

The fifty teenagers from the refugee camps were selected and registered in record time. Because there was no precedent in this kind of program the usual bureaucratic delays were lacking and in about six weeks this initial group was ready for travel. BSC was required to issue an assurance of support for each exchangee during the one-year stay in America, much like the form used in resettlement of refugees except there was emphatic understanding that these were not to be resettled.

In the United States BSC was pushing to secure host homes, and documents were used for this purpose on which the pastor of the church was also asked to sign with the applying family. A separate document had to be secured from the principal of the local high school showing willingness to enroll the student.

Soon after the group of fifty were well on the way of being processed for travel, another new development arose which changed the picture. Fifty German teenagers seemed like a daring project to begin with but an urgent request came for BSC to accept an additional group of forty from one of the German states in the south. James Keim from Pennsylvania State University was working in Württemberg-Baden in the occupation program with rural youth and had earlier negotiated with BSC staff about exchanges. He heard of the plans for the fifty teenagers and became eager to have his territory and program involved in a similar way. The original fifty were refugee children but he worked with the regular and indigenous German farm youths of that state.

Mr. Keim had written some of his friends at Penn State asking if they would find farm homes for some of his youths and they consented. He proceeded to select and prepare forty teenagers for his project but when he announced this number to his friends they threw up their hands in utter dismay and told him they thought he was talking about only five or six. So Mr. Keim had forty teenagers but no place to send them to. In desperation he approached BSC at Frankfurt and inquired if it could not add his group to the program of fifty and make it ninety.

A fifteen-minute call from Frankfurt to Elgin got the consent of W. Harold Row to increase the program by this number. Now there were ninety teenagers being prepared in Germany in two separate groups to be programmed by the Church of the Brethren in America. The first group was to receive travel papers from the US Military Authority to sail on September 14, 1949. They assembled at the staging area at Bremerhaven for final preparation to embarking.

Four days before sailing the group set out for Bremerhaven. Thirty-five of them gathered at Frankfurt to go in a group from there to the staging area. The BSC director of the Frankfurt office met them in the evening at the railroad station as they arrived and took them across the street to the Schumann Snack Bar, a US PX depot, to await the military train to take them on. During this three-hour wait one of the situations arose that somewhat characterized the role of the sponsoring agency throughout the program. It was suppertime and some of these students had had no food since morning.

BSC staff were approved personnel in Germany and were eligible to buy in any PX, and thus carried the necessary military scrip to pay for purchases. It was common practice for

Americans to take a German guest to lunch but how could one take thirty-five?

After some consultation, it was agreed that two BSC staff persons with scrip to pay would take the group through the cafeteria line three or four at a time. When one party had been through and settled at a table with a substantial lunch, a second was escorted down the line, and so the entire thirty-five were fed in the course of about three hours.

Some parents came with their children to this Frankfurt send-off. One could sense deep emotions at parting and their heroic efforts to have complete trust in the project and confidence in BSC that everything would be all right. Many of these youth were able to show a new watch, a camera, or some new items of clothing that had been provided them by family or friends for this great trip. One girl was completely outfitted by the US commanding officer of her area who had known her and her family. The three youths from Berlin were flown in by the empty returning air lift and thus solved that difficult travel arrangement. The entire group at Bremerhaven were fed in the officers' mess, not in the general quarters for the privates. At first eyebrows were raised by some until the program was known and its purpose explained, and then complete acceptance, if not genuine enthusiasm, was expressed by officers and wives with whom the students ate.

The three days at Bremerhaven were spent in getting acquainted, explaining, answering questions, and attempting to project the experiences of the coming year. What an American high school is like, how families live, the value placed on the church by the host family, etc., were among the topics discussed. The Elgin headquarters side of the exchange had done a good job in anticipation of the program and had asked each host family to send a welcoming letter to the student while yet in Germany. These letters were the subject of much comparison among the exchangees and the nature and advantage of each assigned location was much debated. Perhaps most of all, there was felt a need on the part of BSC, and some apprehension on the part of students, to make as clear as possible what it would mean to live in a guest relationship in an American family for one whole year. It is interesting to look back to see that most of the significant aspects of the exchange, at least from the standpoint of the student, were anticipated and discussed even at that early time. However, one of the things later learned was that no amount of briefing could do what the experience itself did.

The day of departure for the first fifty arrived. The *Henry Gibbins,* an army transport, was docked at the pier. It carried about one thousand passengers of returning military personnel to the USA. The boys of the student group, in contrast to their experience at the staging barracks where they ate in the officers' mess, were billeted in a large dormitory area, the same used for returning GI's. They were assigned certain deck duties on the voyage. This was unfortunate, as the military itself admitted, and perhaps somewhat in restitution when the group returned a year later, they were carried on the best air transports available. The girls fared better in guest cabins. And thus on September 14, 1949, at four p.m. the first teenagers sailed from Europe to the United States under the auspices of the occupation forces in Germany and the Church of the Brethren in an experiment that was to prove that high school exchanges were not only possible but perhaps the most productive of all exchanges in long-range intercultural values.

About a month later the second group of forty from Württemberg-Baden came through much the same schedule; the girls were carried on the military transport, the *General Rose,* and the boys on the *General Hodges.* In the meantime, while all this was happening in Germany, BSC stateside was setting up the unprecedented program of family hospitality and high school acceptance for ninety foreign teenagers. We felt that the exchangee should live in the home as much as possible like a son or daughter without violating the real child-parent relationship that had to be maintained in Germany. Parental supervision, work responsibility, spending money, among many other questions, were anticipated and decided by those inexperienced in this kind of business.

But the people involved in the United States were not amateurs in goodwill. While the program became more professional as the years passed, nothing helped more than simple goodwill in making the exchange work. Host families for the most part were middle-class, whereas superior teenagers were selected from a large group of applicants. Sometimes students found themselves in considerably different circumstances, and to a certain extent this was true for all, regardless of the effort to make a suitable choice of host family with comparable interests and economic status.

Upon arrival in the United States, the teenagers were brought to the Brethren Service Center at New Windsor, Maryland, for further orientation and discussion about their placements. Many host families came there to meet their students and take them home in their cars. The church sharing in the sponsorship made special plans to welcome the new guest. One of the host parents took the student to meet the school principal and help arrange for his enrollment. Often a news item in the local paper, with photographs, announced his coming to the community. And so while the first few weeks were overwhelming, the exchangees found themselves surrounded with every conceivable aid to make them welcome and feel at home.

Much of the initial excitement was soon to die down, as the experiences leveled off and the real process of international and intercultural exchange took place. Supervising field-trips were made to families, schools, and exchangees as deemed valuable. Special mailings and written responses from the students were asked, which were shared in a newsletter called *Echo*. These *Echoes* became quite famous documents sharing news, questions, and opinions among families, schools, churches, and students. There was an *Echo* later put out in Europe for the returning exchangees, and visits were made to help resettle them after their return, for this, too, was found to be helpful.

Before the first ninety returned home, an additional four hundred German teenagers were selected and sent to America by the Cultural Affairs Department of the occupation authority. However, only 194 of these were sponsored by the Brethren. By 1952 seven different organizations, including the Church of the Brethren, were sponsoring high school exchanges and these rapidly spread to include many other countries of the world. It became an important program in the International Education Exchange Services of the State Department, which continued for many years to give some financial support to the various teenager exchanges.

While this account seems to credit Brethren for the teenager exchange, very soon other denominations gave it support even while under Brethren administration. After eight program years the interest and participation of other denominations was such that it became right and necessary to make it interdenominational, and so by the program year of 1957-58 six member denominations incorporated and organized to continue the Brethren program under the name of the International Christian Youth Exchange (ICYE).

The program remained at New Windsor for the next two years and then moved to New York under new leadership. It emphasized the direct two-way exchange and came to involve church participation in many of the major countries of the world. An international office was set up in Geneva to facilitate a truly international program. The basic format and purpose of the program has pretty well been maintained in that people, and especially parents, who trust other people, are willing to prove this by the exchange of their children for one year. And as one teenager wrote in the early years of the exchange after her return home, "There is a deep, almost invisible blessing in it."

17. International Work Camps

by Mary Coppock Hammond

The Brethren Service program in Europe utilized a state-side movement among youth to expand its witness to war-weary embittered people by summer projects that truly demonstrated "love in action." They also provided the young people there with an opportunity to restore connections with the world's young people after their long period of isolation during the times of Hitler and war. In the mid-thirties Brethren youth had worked at establishing work camps in areas in the US where real tensions and social conflicts existed. These operated where migrant workers came in for seasonal work and in mining areas. The work camp movement was already then worldwide, because a Swiss pacifist, Pierre Ceresole, began such work in France for European young people in the aftermath of World War I. More than thirty idealistic international voluntary groups were also carrying on programs that were similar.

Brethren Service developed its international work camp programs with all of its staff personnel participating in the year-round planning and the material aid workers allocated to staff the projects for an eight-week period during the summer. There is a simple philosophical statement upon which all such camps operate: tensions are overcome only when physical work is undertaken by all factions in a common cause for improving economic conditions in that area with all sides cooperating. Although many such projects were attempted, those sponsored by Brethren made a total impact on the area and upon each volunteer who chose to serve in them.

The BSC camps enabled Brethren youth to view the whole service program in that fifty to one hundred of them were accepted and scattered among four to ten projects. The annual plans offered no two camps where the social problem was comparable nor was the seminar topic exactly the same.

The major tension point in West Berlin, in West Germany's three zones, and in Austria was the conflict between the local citizens and the refugees who were dumped upon them by international treaties. In Italy, there was the struggle for the Protestant youth to have contact with the world's Protestant movement. In Greece, the people were numbed by their long experiences with war and internal conflicts; their own young people were so apathetic that the leaven of meeting foreign, caring, young people awakened them to an awareness of the fact that all young people who worked in humble local situations for social and economic betterment improved the climate for international understanding. Occasionally, as in Poland and West Berlin, the tension was in the struggle of the Communists to implement their doctrine by persuasion and force.

In all areas there was local conflict between the young people and the older generations who had become bitter and cynical. These projects successfully demonstrated that people of all colors, creeds, and political doctrines could work together and in such a short time establish a lasting sense of community, and thus broaden the self-help programs planned by local authorities and refugee leaders. These projects had bogged down because most uprooted refugees desired to return to their own countries and because so much had already happened to them due to circumstances beyond their control that they were pessimistic about any of their efforts really benefitting them.

Naturally, to establish such projects abroad brought difficulties that our stateside projects could not even imagine. There was an endless amount of red tape to overcome just to assist with the preparation of passports and visas. At times, it seemed that the language barrier was insurmountable. Our application blanks clearly stated that no one should apply unless he or she spoke one of the two "official" camp languages. One was always English, and the second, the native tongue of the site of the camp. Our behind-the-scenes goal of seminar discussions taking place "off the work project" necessitated that the participants would have to be articulate to offer ideas for others to consider and discuss. Then, when one was to return to his own home he would have for his lifetime a whole new set of values from which to view problems in his own situation. The Brethren projects did not desire to create a worldwide professional voluntary service permanent group but rather to have each return to his own community where his new awareness would strengthen the most worthwhile things being done locally.

As the program developed over the years, the so-called "director" of each project usually was selected from stateside suggestions according to the discussion topic for each project. Most of them also paid their own expenses as there was little support for the total international work camp program in the cramped budget of an agency that attempted to do so many types of work to "restore, rehabilitate, reconstruct, and reconcile" former enemies. Yet, in each project the director, or the experienced BSC staff member, relieved of his regular program for camp duration by the cooperation of the total staff, found in each group a nucleus of five or six who were in on the advance plans for the projects.

Midpoint in the program, many BVS workers served as "head-sisters," assistant directors, and some in the second summer of their term were full directors of these camps. When supplies were adequate, BSC offered food subsidies for each project and transported food to campsites. They also usually provided "truck-transportation-swaps" of young people too poor to pay their own transportation, but whose presence would indelibly alter the experiences of the more affluent young people who came in from countries that were not suffering the aftermath of war.

The very openness of our recruitment policies realistically tested the idealism of our youth in the most trying circumstances. Avowed Nazis and undercover Communists at times tried to wreck our purposes. It was the first time many of our own youth encountered agnosticism and atheism embodied in humanistic individuals. But the possibility of building a sense of community was truly realized. Many who came to scoff had their own outlook transformed by the miracle of an understanding developed by the accomplishment of a constructive physical project amidst the obvious chaotic destruction of war and the brokenness of the human beings. These were destined to remain in that locality, whereas the volunteers could return to pick up the fortunate threads of their own lives.

Many camps went through similar phases which attest to the validity of the whole work camp philosophy. All who came first put their best feet forward; all came prepared to accept others from varying backgrounds; all came confident of their own abilities to do something to alleviate the miseries of others. Since the total impact of the camps was also to have lasting good effects on tense groups of the community, time had to be structured so that certain time allotments were closed to the surrounding community allowing participants to explore local problems with more detachment than when community members were present.

Intellectually, the visiting campers were sincere in wanting to participate in such a situation. Emotionally, a Dutch girl was not prepared to even associate with a "still-Nazi German." Emotionally, the shame and guilt of German Christian youth for the sins of their nation often made them supersensitive to a discussion of prewar times in European countries. Likewise, our own youth seemed to hold the people responsible somehow, yet did not want themselves to accept responsibility for the destruction rained on civilians by allied nations. Even those who had themselves suffered from the Nazi regime because their parents openly opposed Hitler were by no means ready to accept a Jew as a daily companion. Participants whose faith was not tested in their home communities found that quietly demonstrating it took more self-discipline and more daily prayer than an extremely busy day provided.

The camps did operate democratically, and although advance contacts had been made to insure truly stimulating seminars, each group set its own work schedule and voted on which contacts to pursue and which places to visit during their free time. Americans were asked not to live above the economic status of the community, so they could meet as equals and not as do-gooders whose material affluence would alienate them from other participants. As in all unit-type stateside projects, directors could always sense a crisis, but in most instances such crises—if overcome by a democratic Christian approach—built a deeper spirit of fellowship than had our camps not been so open. The small nucleus in each camp prayed together or met in free time if the whole camp did not program daily devotions or religious discussions. The small group aimed to reach the camper "the furthest out" by including him in their love and concern even when his ideas or actions were unpopular with the group. Following camp, those in between the one farthest out and the planning nucleus were often the ones most transformed by such an experience.

Since great effort had been made before camp opened to have the locality informed of the plans, naturally the jobs attempted were by no means glamorous. Unemployment in postwar Europe was prevalent, and the work done must never take paying jobs from local people. Labor codes meant that American know-how and do-it-yourself ideas must be approved by local officials who had to guarantee that local regulations were met. One of the side benefits for many directors was the reluctant admission by skilled, local, work-project advisors that untrained, willing, idealistic youth could truly do a piece of work that met all standards. Such men were often assigned to us by government officials, and even these paid inspectors later helped organize volunteer workers to do jobs which helped stretch the budgets of orphanages, refugee camps, hospitals, and church-supported projects.

In the latter period of BSC sponsorship staff members and offices were flooded with requests for assistance on projects. This was indeed a reversal from what the initiators of the program found when they laboriously persuaded the World's YMCA and other groups to allow international groups to assume the cleanup and unskilled labor, so that meagre budgets could get prewar services functioning again. Conscientious efforts were made to select projects that would serve many functions. If the director of a refugee camp would approve a budget that provided the money for a chapel for worship, then that director was encouraged to adapt plans so that the chapel could serve as a social hall where refugees could escape the confines of their limited living quarters. Many such chapels became real camp community service centers rather than only places of worship.

Work camps did help build rural retreat houses for church youth, but the program put into effect was to make their retreats small work camps to expand the facilities, and to bring together diverse groups so that the retreats became tools of reconciliation. Excavating basements for refugee housing projects got the whole self-help project under way, but when the refugees and local inhabitants knew that a total of work camp hours made the down payment for an apartment for a widow or a disabled person, local refugee and citizen groups continued to volunteer labor for refugees who could not physically make the down payment for their housing in money or labor. Such self-help projects in postwar Europe are a real monument to the success of international youth projects.

Nearly half of our camps were located in institutions where a lighter work schedule was adopted so that the volunteers could also assist in caring for patients or work with handcrafts. Both the physical contribution and the social-service assistance were reasons why certain volunteers selected such projects. A few projects had lighter work schedules so that the seminar function could be expanded. A few projects brought theological students of many countries together.

One West Berlin seminar on "Communism and Christianity" actually observed a World Communist Confederation assembly across the street. Dr. Floyd E. Mallott, who directed the study side of that international work camp seminar, had informed us in advance that it was not necessary to go to such a spot for such a purpose, that he could do the same seminar in Chicago or in Timbuctoo. But, when it ended, he reinforced the planners' beliefs that only on the spot can one get the total perspective of a problem. Many of our participants had prior experience in international study seminars or later participated in them. All responded that the combination work camp-international seminar was the type of life-experience that either alone could not offer.

Some twenty years later vivid memories attest to the lifelong effect of my own time as a participant in a project, the director of another, and as a BSC staff member who attended the evaluation conferences of work camp sponsoring groups: I recall the Austrian Jewish secretary who wept at the breakup of camp and said that until she participated in the fellowship of that group, she had vowed never to care enough for anyone to shed a tear; she had shed so many in her girlhood over the fate of her people. I remember the boy who would not even jokingly use a term like "chopping off heads" because he informed us Americans that he had seen heads roll in the street. Also the Nazi participant in a fun night for the community in the last week of camp dressed as an American cowboy singing "Home on the Range" with a terrible accent. And the Yugoslavian refugee boy who spent spare time memorizing the Bible because the time might come in the future as it had in his

Christian parents' lives when the only Scripture they had to pass on to their children in the concentration camp was what they had had in their heads.

Memories include two different camps that had suicide attempts in the final week because the refugee participants could not bear for it to end when they did not know their own future. I remember the girl who had spent her war years in a Japanese concentration camp and who, when a camper criticized the camp food, remarked that it was much better than the worm-infested food that she had had to survive on during the war.

The closing of camp often included a voluntary "communion," and some asked to participate with just a partial belief which they illustrated by the verse: "Lord, I believe. Help my unbelief." Later we received letters indicating that some had resumed their attendance at church services of their own faith because they wanted to nourish the seed of faith established by participation in such a group. Some foreign friends I met during these camps have since visited me. Others still exchange letters with me. And it is still a reward when the phone rings and someone traveling Interstate 75 calls to schedule a visit to reminisce about our experiences.

The example of BSC and other international voluntary agencies served to arouse other Christian denominations to engage in broad social work at home and abroad. VISTA and Peace Corps programs were organized on guidelines suggested by the many who engaged in these earlier endeavors.

That the world still has immense problems does not detract from the efforts to meet problems. For everyone who participated, there is a deep, inner assurance that the direction in which we worked in these programs was the direction that would have eliminated some of our problems of today had only enough of the world's people experienced this sense of community. A lifetime pursuing similar goals is more rewarding than a mere existence.

Bibliographical Notes

by Donald F. Durnbaugh

No comprehensive history of the activities of BSC has been written. The most complete study yet made is Roger E. Sappington, "The Development of Social Policy in the Church of the Brethren: 1908-1958," a doctoral dissertation written at Duke University (1959), published in shortened form as *Brethren Social Policy, 1908-1958* (Elgin, 1961). The development, expansion, consolidation, and retrenchment of BSC make up a large part of the narrative. It is based on close examination of pertinent Brethren records, primarily at denominational headquarters in Elgin, Illinois. Sappington's interpretation was questioned, in part, by W. Harold Row, executive secretary of BSC after 1948, because of the emphasis placed on the roles of a few key leaders, especially M. R. Zigler, and because non-Brethren records were not consulted in the course of the study. Row himself attempted to lay out the theological foundation for Brethren Service in two articles, "The Historical and Theological Bases of Social Welfare in the Church of the Brethren," *Brethren Life and Thought,* 1 (Spring 1956), 7-13—first published in E. T. Bachmann, ed., *The Activating Concern* (New York, 1955), 11-17—and "The Brethren and Biblical Ethics," *The Adventurous Future,* ed. Paul H. Bowman (Elgin, 1959), 132-41. Unfortunately Row's untimely death in 1971 precluded a larger assessment of Brethren Service work.

Lorell Weiss made two important contributions to the topic. His *Ten Years of Brethren Service* (Elgin, [1951]) is an excellent brief summary of the first decade following formal organization of BSC in 1941. In order to avoid invidious choices, he refrained from using any names of BSC staff and volunteers. A longer study was accepted as a doctoral dissertation by the University of Southern California in 1957; the title "Socio-Psychological Factors in the Pacifism of the Church of the Brethren During the Second World War" fails to reveal that the text includes a well-balanced and analytical description of the full range of Brethren Service activity from the beginning to the post-war years.

A brief discussion of the importance of Brethren Service in the life of the denomination is found in Floyd E. Mallott, *Studies in Brethren History* (Elgin, 1954). An unusually extensive treatment was incorporated in Elmer Q. Gleim, *Change and Challenge: A History of the Church of the Brethren in the Southern District of Pennsylvania, 1940-1972* (Harrisburg, 1973).

The first years of BSC's life were preempted by the emergency caused by governmental conscription prior to and during World War II. BSC leaders were determined to help provide better options for CO's than those obtaining in 1917-18. The initiation and administration of CPS is described by one of the central figures in Rufus D. Bowman, *The Church of the Brethren and War, 1708-1941* (Elgin, 1944); this is now available in reprint from Garland Publishers, Inc. (New York, 1971) with a new introduction by D. F. Durnbaugh. Some additional information is found in Bowman's study guide, *Seventy Times Seven* (Elgin, 1945). The Brethren CPS program was competently studied in the well-documented book by Leslie Eisan, *Pathways of Peace* (Elgin, 1948). More personal testimony is given in William Stafford, *Down in My Heart* (Elgin, 1947), reprinted in 1971.

The official government account is Neal M. Wherry, *Conscientious Objection,* Special Monograph No. 11 (Washington, D. C., 1950), with one volume of text and a second of documents. The most thorough study is Mulford Q. Sibley and Philip E. Jacob, *Conscription of Conscience: The American State and the Conscientious Objector, 1940-1947* (Ithaca, 1952); interestingly the authors differed diametrically on the issue of the rightness of cooperation by the historic peace churches with the Selective Service system. The best overall study of pacifism of the period, Lawrence S. Wittner, *Rebels Against War: The American Peace Movement, 1941-1960* (New York, 1969), has a section on CPS, which, while balanced, is critical of the experiment. The discussion in Peter Brock, *Twentieth-Century Pacifism* (New York, 1970), tends to be more positive in its appraisal.

What was perhaps the single most dramatic project of

CPS, the starvation unit at the University of Minnesota, was thoroughly publicized. Volunteer CO's went on strictly-controlled hunger diets to enable the scientific study of the effects of undernourishment and the best means of restoration. The book by Harold S. Guetzkow and Paul H. Bowman, *Men and Hunger* (Elgin, 1946) was written from the viewpoint of the participants. The scientific results are presented in Ancel Keys and others, *Experimental Starvation in Man* (Minneapolis, 1945) and the two-volume *The Biology of Human Starvation* (Minneapolis, 1950).

Relief and rehabilitation projects have received considerable attention. Those with particular reference to Brethren activity include: Harold E. Fey, *Cooperation in Compassion: The Story of Church World Service* (New York, 1966); Eileen Egan and Elizabeth Clark Reiss, *Transfigured Night: The CRALOG Experience* (Philadelphia, 1964); and Edgar H. S. Chandler, *The High Tower of Refuge* (New York, 1959), written by the director of the service to refugees of WCC. H. B. Allen, *Rural Reconstruction in Action* (Ithaca, 1953), gives brief mention to the first Heifer Project shipment to Europe, six bulls sent to Greece for an artificial insemination clinic sponsored by the Near East Foundation. A British journalist, Robert Kee, provides a very personal account of the problems which confronted BSC and other voluntary agencies in refugee resettlement in *Refugee World* (London, 1961); the author includes a long conversation with a physician at Thalham tubercular sanitorium in Upper Austria which Brethren Service workers were instrumental in starting. The chapter by Geoffrey Murray, "Joint Service as an Instrument of Renewal" in *A History of the Ecumenical Movement, Volume 2: 1948-1968,* ed. Harold E. Fey (Philadelphia, 1970), though sparse in mention of the Brethren, provides helpful information on programs with which and countries in which BSC worked.

The China tractor unit is described in the mimeographed report by Howard Sollenberger and Wendell Flory, *History of the UNRRA-Brethren Service Unit* [Elgin, 1947]. The team was mentioned favorably in the two-volume study, George Woodbridge, *UNRRA: The History of the United Nation's Relief and Rehabilitation Administration* (New York, 1950). Not surprisingly, the earthy fascination of the Heifer Project has found much reporting, primarily in articles. Probably the best account is that of Kermit Eby in the chapter "Unto the Least of These." in *The God in You* (Chicago, 1954).

The little-known story of Brethren aid to Japanese Americans forced from their West Coast homes in World War II hysteria was written up as the project was operating by Richard Burger, "The Trends Toward and Causes of the Evacuation of American Citizens of Japanese Ancestry and the History and Functions of the Brethren Hostel," unpublished B.D. thesis, Bethany Biblical Seminary (1945); the later achievements in Chicago and New York are not covered. The administrator of WRA, Dillon S. Myer, wrote of his experiences in *Uprooted Americans* (Tucson, 1971); he mentions the aid of voluntary agencies in relocating inmates of the interment camps without referring specifically to BSC.

The experience of BSC in Austria has been carefully studied. Two research papers were prepared for courses in church history at Bethany Theological Seminary: Ralph E. Smeltzer, "The History of Brethren Service in Austria, From Its Beginning (November, 1946) to July, 1949" (1949); and Merlin G. Shull, "History of the Brethren Service Commission in Austria, With Special Emphasis on the Span From the Summer of 1950 to the Summer of 1953" (1953). Another study was compiled by a non-Brethren volunteer: Eleanor Williamson, "Brethren Service in Austria, 1947-1958" (1958).

Two symposia have been published on the Brethren Volunteer Service program, one after ten years of activity, another after twenty years, both in *Brethren Life and Thought:* 3 (Summer 1958) and 13 (Autumn 1968). The related program of alternative service was analyzed in two theses: Leland Wilson, "A Sociological Study of the Church of the Brethren Men in Alternative Service," unpublished M.A. thesis, University of Kansas (1957); and Robert B. Blair, "Role Performance and Personality Characteristics of Sixty-One Alternative Service Volunteers in the Church of the Brethren," unpublished M.A. thesis, Northwestern University (1967).

Besides these materials, there is a vast amount of information in the *Gospel Messenger* (later *Messenger*), which for many years had a regular Brethren Service section, in booklets and pamphlets published at Elgin, and in special news bulletins such as the *Brethren Service News* (1945-66).

A Selective Index of Persons and Subjects

A Selective Index

A Selective Index

A Selective Index